I WANTED TO BE...

SO WHAT WAS I D
IN MOOSE JAW?

BY RAY ST. GERMAIN

Pemmican Publications Inc. gratefully acknowledges the assistance accorded to its publishing program by the Manitoba Arts Council, the Canada Arts Council and the Government of Canada through the Book Publishing Industry Development Program (BPIDP) for our publishing activities.

Printed and Bound in Canada.
The Prolific Group

Book Cover – Relish Design
Editorial – Donna Gamache, Diane Ramsay and Glory St. Germain
Layout and Design – Diane Ramsay

Library and Archives Canada Cataloguing in Publication
St. Germain, Ray
I wanted to be Elvis, so what was I doing in Moose Jaw? / Ray St.Germain.
Autobiography.
ISBN 1-894717-32-5
1. St. Germain, Ray. 2. Country musicians--Canada--Biography.
3. Television personalities--Canada--Biography. 4. Métis--Manitoba--Biography.
I. Title.
ML420.S139A3 2005   782.421642'092   C2005-907519-8

 Pemmican Publications Inc.

150 Henry Ave
Winnipeg, MB   R3B 0J7
PH: 204.589.6346
Fax: 204.589.2063
Website: www.pemmican.mb.ca
Email: pemmicanpublications@hotmail.com

Disclaimer

Due to the large number of names,

people, places, bands, etc.,

we wish to apologize for any misspelling

of any of the above, should there be any.

Dedication

To my wife, Glory,

my children and grandchildren,

siblings and their children

and my mom.

Prologue

Well, here it is. The book I've been threatening to write! I decided to do this because every time a subject comes up in a conversation, I usually have a story that I've heard about or have lived through a similar experience.

That's because I have been an entertainer all my life and have traveled most of Canada including the Arctic Circle, Germany, Israel and Cyprus. During this time I have appeared on more than 500 network television shows as a singing host for the CBC and Global Television Network in Canada. I've made many recordings but no big hits. I've played pubs, clubs, lounges, fairs, rodeos, festivals and wherever they needed entertainment, including countless charity gigs… I have a lot of mugs.

As an entertainer, you experience many emotions on a gig or during a three-minute song. It depends where you are singing, for whom and if the band likes the song or even you.

By the way, most musicians hate singers. The reason is simple. A good musician puts in many hours practicing his or her axe and ends up playing back up to a singer with a natural voice, who spends little time looking after their voice and then receives all the applause. The singer then begs the audience for a little applause for the band. That's why most musicians learn to sing.

Table of Contents

Chapter 1 – The Beginning   1

Chapter 2 – St. Germain Genealogy   3

Chapter 3 - Lenny Breau (Jazz Legend)   7

Chapter 4 – Television   13

Chapter 5 – Toronto 1959   15

Chapter 6 – More Television   19

Chapter 7 – Chan's Moon Room Cabaret   21

Chapter 8 – Northern Manitoba Tours   25

Chapter 9 – The Journals   27

Chapter 10 - Anne Murray and Re-uniting with Hal Lone Pine   31

Chapter 11 – Back to Toronto   33

Chapter 12 – The Sting – 1975   37

Chapter 13 – Brian Whyte my half-brother   39

Chapter 14 – The Lounge   41

Chapter 15 – Jimmy King   43

Chapter 16 –   Ray St. Germain Country/Big Sky Country   45

Chapter 17 –   The Farm   49

Chapter 18 –   Overseas Tour – 1983   51

Chapter 19 – Canadian Armed Forces Tour – 1987   57

Chapter 20 – Ramada Inn   59

Chapter 21 – I Quit the Road   61

Epilogue   65

Major Awards   67

Discography   71

Pictures   73

Chapter 1
The Beginning

*1958 – Ray in front of
27 St. Michaels Road*

I was born July 29, 1940 in St. Vital, a suburb of Winnipeg, Manitoba, Canada. My mother was Hilda Dona Ducharme and my dad Simon Adrian St. Germain. Dad built a house at 27 St. Michael's Road in St. Vital after he got out of the army. My siblings include Val, Judy, Jesse and a half-brother, Brian Whyte. Growing up my siblings and I didn't know we were Metis. My mom and dad decided not to tell us to protect us from the prejudice that existed back then and in some cases, still exists today. They didn't want us to have to deal with being called Half-breeds. So, we grew up thinking we were French with Scottish mixed in from my Grandma Jesse Ducharme whose maiden name was McDougall.

Actually, most Metis were still hiding their identity because of the horrible discrimination. If you could get away with having light skin you were lucky. If you had brown skin like my dad and his brothers you always had grief, especially in the Armed Forces or downtown Winnipeg. By the way, I grew up believing they had brown skin because they worked outside all year round and they were well tanned.

*Grandma Alphonse St. Germain and Grandpa
Wilfred (George) St. Germain
Approximately 1920*

My grandparents, on my dad's side, lived at Lot 139 St. Mary's Road in St. Vital. It was located on the south side of Winnipeg. That area was also known as a Metis community or, where the Half-Breeds lived.

My grandparents on my mother's side, Jesse and Joe Ducharme, lived across the street from us at 24 St. Michael's Road. Grandpa Ducharme was a Metis from the Craig Siding area, now known as St. Rita. Grandma Ducharme insisted there wasn't a drop of Indian blood in her.

I'll get more into my family a little later in the book.

1948 – Grandpa Joe Ducharme, Val (Ray's sister) and Ray

1955 – Ray, fifteen years old

When I was fourteen, in 1954, I joined a country band by the name of "The Rhythm Ranch Boys." Len Fairchuk was the bandleader and played the fiddle. Roy DeLaRonde played the guitar and sang. The drummer, I believe was Dennis Willows. I was hired to play accordion and sing. We rehearsed at Roy's place after school and played weekends at dances out of town. When I started singing Elvis songs and other rock & roll numbers that were all the craze, "the new music for kids only," Roy taught me how to play the guitar. He said I would probably hurt myself jumping and shaking all over the stage with an accordion on. After all, Elvis played guitar.

I also competed on the CJOB Western Hour, a radio show broadcast live every Saturday from Dominion Theatre in Winnipeg, where the Fairmount Hotel now stands. It was an amateur show for western singers. The name "Country Singer" wasn't used back then. George "Hank" McCloy was the M.C. and the band, I believe was the *Western Seven.* Later it was *Glen Frain and his Buckaroos.* The singers would audition at noon and three were picked to compete against the reigning "King or Queen of the Saddle." The number of votes that were mailed in determined the winner and the winner was announced the next week.

I went down to audition week after week after week. Sometimes I would be chosen to compete. I never won, but the experience I was getting every week performing before a live audience was invaluable. By the way, the rest of the show was made up of seasoned, well-known singers as guests. Some of the names I recall were Smokey Ferlin, Eddy Laham, Bob Bedard, Ray Drayne, and one of the best singers I ever heard, even to this day, Art Young.

The show later moved to the Starland Theatre on Main Street and playing steel guitar in Glen Frain's band was none other then a very young Ron Halldorson, who went on to fame as one of the best musicians this town produced. Oh, and by the way, I was now one of the guest singers. I guess they decided enough was enough of me coming down every week trying to compete. By this time I had built a following and I was starting to be known as "Winnipeg's Elvis Presley".

And get this, my youngest sister, Judy, auditioned *once*, got on and became "Queen of the Saddle." She still reminds me to this day.

Chapter 2
St. Germain Genealogy

1. *Francois Brisard* married Marie Benoist – The French information says: St.-Germain-Du Seudre Arrondissement Jonzac Saintonge-Charente-Maritime France. The nearest date I can find is 1706 when he came over to Quebec as a solider in the French Army.

2. *Jean Brisard Dit St. Germain* (Soldat, Cie La Durantaye) married Marie-Anee Degerlaise, daughter of Jean-Jeanne Trudel. There is a date of 1714-03-04, Trois Rivieres QC. This date is either for birth or marriage.

3. *Alex Brisard Dit St-Germain,* 1751-08-23 Maskinonge QC, married Margaret Vanasse-Sebastien, daughter of Suz. Lupien and Sebastien.

4. *Alexis St. Germian,* 1779-10-18 Louiseville Q.C. married Louise Chabot, daughter of Joseph-Fel. Petitclerc. (at this point, the name Brisard no longer appears, that explains why many people with the name St. Germain are not related. They may be called Benoist of St. Germain in France and just St. Germain when they headed west.)

5. *Joseph St. Germain* born 1796 in Quebec. Another date of 1833-11-19 St. Boniface, Manitoba is probably the date of marriage to Marie Cadotte, daughter of Laurent-Maskegonne

6. *Joseph St. Germian,* ca1845 St. Boniface, Manitoba married Anne McGilvray daughter of Samuel-Therese Roy. This is the Joseph St. Germain Louis Riel refers to in his letters to his mother while in exile in Montana. He always says hello to his good friend and warns him of surveyors cheating the measurement of lands.

7. *Simon St. Germain* born-1856 in St. Vital and died May 25, 1940, buried in St. Norbert cemetery on October 8th, 1878. He married Rose Hamelin, daughter of Joseph-Josephte Sayer. He was a St. Vital counselor and reeve, an immigrant officer, a charter member of the union society of St. Joseph, secretary and president.

St. Germain school was built across from his home. He was named Chairman of the Board in the school district he created. In 1987 a new French immersion school was built in St. Vital and named after him. They had six sons and three daughters.

Napoleon and Joachem who lived in St. Vital
Maxim who lived in Togo, Saskatchewan
Ralph who lived in Port Arthur
Ernest and Samuel – St. Vital, Lot 139 St. Mary's Road, (Simon's Home) The two oldest boys Joachem and Ernest stayed on the farm to work it while the younger children went on to higher education.

THREE DAUGHTERS

Ida Carrier – St. Vital and later Pine Falls, Manitoba
Olive Deslauriers – Winnipeg

Lucie – a nun who died at Cross Lake, Manitoba

He had at the time of his death 21 grandchildren and nine great grandchildren

8. *Joachem St. Germain* born July 25th, 1881 married Olivine Normand August 9th, 1908 in St. Norbert. Olivine was born May 15th, 1890.

He worked as a labourer all his life. He used to dig house basements with a shovel! They lived at lot 139 St. Mary's Road, at the back of his father's house. They had four sons.

Alphonse – married Rose, worked at Artic Ice – Boux Plastering, he had one son – *Roland,* three daughters – *Lucille, Terry and Germaine.* He died of cancer

Wilfred – labourer – Artic Ice – never married – served in the Army. He died of cancer.

Urban – Labourer – never married – served in the Army, went overseas and fathered a son in Germany. He was called the *Bull of St. Vital* because of his love for fighting. He died of cancer.

Simon Adrian St. Germain – Died of Alzheimers.

9. *Simon Adrian St. Germain* (The Champ) – born August 12th, 1914 and Dona Hilda Ducharme born March 29th, 1923, daughter of Joseph Ducharme and Jesse McDougall of Que'Apple Valley, Saskatchewan, married on Saturday, October 7th, 1939 at 7:30 AM in St. Emile Church on St. Anne's Road in St. Vital. Roman Catholic priest father Brunette performed the ceremony. Mr. Yablonski, who owned the grocery store near Komoroski Grocery Store on St. Mary's Road drove them to the church

in his old Model T car. They rented a small house at 1090 St. Mary's Road. (between St. Micheal's Road and Arden) for $10 a month.

They had two sons, Raymond and Jesse and two daughters Valerie and Judy. Simon also fathered another son, Brian Whyte, four years before he married Dona Hilda.

Simon served in the Army during the Second World War and was stationed in Lethbridge, Alberta as a guard for German prisoners.

He was an amateur boxer (middleweight). He worked as a greens keeper for the Windsor Park Golf Course. He rode the rails to find work out west. He used to swim to his job across the Red River in St. Vital with his clothes tied on top of his head.

He worked for Canada Packers for over 40 years on the docks as a shipper and receiver. He also drove long haul trucking for the packers and worked on the killing floor, but the hardest of all was shaking hides.

When he retired, he went to work as a security guard and as a truck driver for Eaton's.

He built two houses, 27 St. Micheal's Road and his present one at 17 Abbotsford Crescent, both in St. Vital.

Further Information Gathered:

#5. Joseph St. Germain – son of Alexis Brisard and Louise Chabotte married Marie Cadotte, daughter of Laurent-Suzanne Maskegonne on November 19th, 1833 in St. Boniface, Manitoba. Marie

was born in 1796 and baptized November 18th, 1834. They had three sons.

#6. Joseph St. Germain – born in 1820 and was baptized April 13th, 1834. Married Anne McGilvrey who was born in 1826 and was the daughter of Samuel and Therese Roy. They had ten children.

The ten children are:

Joseph – born April 27th, 1846 in St. Boniface

Frederic – born June 1st, 1850 in St. Norbert

Augustine – born in October in St. Norbert

Anne – born 1848 – married Damase Perreault son of Jean Baptiste and Marie Charron/Ducharme on June 25th, 1868.

Julie – born 1851, died October 11th, 1863 in St. Norbert

Simon – born May 28th, 1859. Reference material also says May 30th, 1859 St. Norbert, Frs. Roy and Isabelle Lafrenier (possibly Godparents)

Alexandre – born December 31st, 1861, baptized January 1st, 1862 at St. Norbert, Manitoba – Jos. St. Germain – Nancy Gladu (possibly Godparents)

M. Virginie – born January 15th, 1864-baptised same day at St. Norbert.

Alfred – born June 20th, 1866 baptised June 21st, 1866 St. Norbert, Manitoba – Martin Jerome – Annie St. Germain (possibly godparents)

Ida – born 1868 died April 16th, 1873 in St. Norbert

Other Information

Pierre St. Germain – born 1830 St. Norbert, Manitoba

Augustine St. Germain – born November 28th, 1824, married Josephte
Pierre St. Germain – interpreter for the copper Indians

Hired at Ft. Resolution July 24th, 1820, St. Germain proved to be the best hunter, the most intelligent interpreter and had the most influence with the Indians. He accompanied Back and Hood to the Coppermine River (Point Lake) August 29th to September 10th, 1820. When supplies arrived at Fort Providence, he led eight voyageurs to get them, leaving November 28th, 1820. Seven of them arrived back at Fort Enterprise on January 15th, 1821 with two kegs of run, one barrel of powder, sixty pounds of ball, two rolls of tobacco and some clothing. Each man carrying sixty to ninety pounds; St. Germain returned January 27th, bringing the two Eskimos, Augustus and Junius.

Strong, resourceful, practical and a man of great stamina, he ferried Franklin across Belanger Rapids on September 14th. The disastrous and dispiriting nine-day delay in crossing the icy Coppermine River finally ended on October 4th, 1821 when he completed a little cockleshell canoe out of fragments of painted canvas in which the officers wrapped their bedding. The next day he was chosen to go with Back, Beauparlant and Solomon Belanger to obtain the assistance expected at Fort Enterprise. When the fort was deserted, they went on a further day's travel to Roundrock Lake, where they camped from October 14th to 30th. It was St. Germain who reached Akaitcho's camp on November 3rd, sending them with food to the dying men at Fort Enterprise.

There are at least twelve references to Pierre throughout the journal. Another book entitled *"The Fate of Franklin"* by Roderic Owen refers to Pierre at least ten times.

Frederic St. Germain – Son of Augustine St. Germain ca 1824 and Josephte Primeau was born in St. Norbert, Manitoba on December 3rd, 1852 and died at Batoche, Saskatchewan on August 21st, 1953 (100 yrs. old). He married Melanie Parenteau, daughter of Pierre and Marianne Caron who was born in 1853 at St. Norbert, Manitoba and died at Batoche in 1951 (98 years old).

Note: Augustine was the son of Joseph (#5) and brother of Joseph (#6)

They had nine children:

Alexandre - baptised 1880
William – baptised 1877
Florestine – baptised 1882
Raoul – married Justine Caron, daughter of Patrice and Eleonore on August 16th, 1921 at Batoche, Saskatchewan. He died in 1973.
Ernest – no information available
Marguerite – married Eugene Caron
Joseph (Caron?) – married Marguerite Gervais
Corrine – no information available
Alfred – married Justine Laplante
Pierre - married Sara Duchene
Charles - married Angelique Lafournaise
Veronique - married Moise Parenteau
Joseph, Francois, Marguerite, Baptiste and Isabelle – no information available

Frederic: at Lethbridge 1900-01 re-scrip claim

Chapter 3
Lenny Breau (Jazz Legend)

I first met Lenny Breau when I was sixteen. He was fifteen and the son of country music legends Hal Lone Pine and Betty Cody. The Lone Pine show came to Winnipeg in 1956 to work on CKY Radio and perform shows in and around the listening area. They would tape shows to be played every morning at 7:00A.M, six days a week. They would announce the names of the towns they would be playing at on the show.

Lone Pine and his family show came from Bangor, Maine where they had become stars in the country music field. He was host of the WWVA Wheeling, West Virginia Jamboree, which at the time was as big as the Grand Ole Opry on WSM out of Nashville. He and Betty were written up many times in the *Country Music Round-up Magazine* which sold all over the world and was the *People Magazine* of its time for lovers of country & western music. Their hit recordings included "I Heard The Bluebirds Sing" (the original) "Apple Blossom Time in Annapolis Valley" and many others. Hal Lone Pine's real name was Harold Breau. At one time he had also been the host of the *Louisiana Hayride,* which was bigger than the *Grand Ole Opry.*

Lenny was billed as Lone Pine Jr., "The Wizard of the Guitar." And even at fifteen, he was. His idol, like many other guitar players, was Chet Atkins. The only difference between Lenny and other guitar players of any age was that he could play all Chet's songs note for note from memory. He couldn't read music!

For those of you who don't know how Chet plays, I'll try to explain. With a thumb pick he would play notes and rhythm on the thicker strings with a tic-tic sound, while picking out a melody on the rest of the strings

CKY Caravan – 1956
Jim Daughtry, Jack Paget, Betty Cody, Hal Lone Pine and Lone Pine Jr. (Lenny Breau)

with the remaining fingers on his right hand. It's very hard to explain and even harder to do. Not many players can master the Chet Atkins' style. But Lenny Breau, at fifteen years of age, could.

I was singing every weekend at the Rainbow Dance Gardens with a country group and doing Elvis impersonations. The Rainbow was located in downtown Winnipeg and on the second floor. The bandstand was elevated and nicely lit but you could still see out onto the dance floor and into the booths that surrounded it. Wally Diduck was on fiddle, Corky Taylor on steel, Mel Kreston on drums, our band leader Wally Faryon on accordion and me on rhythm guitar. We all listened to the Lone Pine Show on the radio and were aware that they were big stars from the U.S.A. What we didn't realize was that getting a radio show up in Canada and traveling to small towns to perform was kind of the last leg for fading U.S. recording stars. But it didn't matter to us. They had been *there*! (Wherever *there* was.)

The show was called the *CKY Caravan* starring "Hal Lone Pine and Betty Cody featuring The Guitar Wizard, 14-year-old Lone Pine Jr." The posters read that too, so Lenny stayed fourteen until the posters ran out.

One night while we were on stage playing, someone came running up and said that Lone Pine, Betty Cody and their son, Lone Pine Jr. had come into the dance hall and were sitting at a booth listening to us. Oh my God! We all started to check the tuning on our instruments. Even the accordion player was checking octaves on his accordion. We all wished we were playing with somebody better. The band wished they had a better singer. Then it happened. A written request for me to sing an Elvis song from Hal Lone Pine himself!

'Oh Lord!' I thought to myself. 'How do I tell our bandleader accordionist to lay out without getting fired?' I used to play accordion and do Elvis when I was fourteen, but I couldn't jump all over the stage without falling down. Someone finally told me it looked silly and that I was going to seriously injure myself if I didn't learn guitar. Besides, Elvis didn't have an accordion in his band. Self-preservation prevailed and I didn't say anything. I started to sing "Hound Dog" and the accordion pumped away.

When I was finished we took a break and Lone Pine called me over to his booth. I walked over with my heart pumping a mile a minute. I reached his table and felt like I was going to faint. I had never met a real singing radio star before. I blurted out, "Hi, Mr. Lone." He said, "Just call me Pine. Sit down and join us." He introduced me to his wife, Betty, and his son, Lenny. Lenny? I thought his name was Lone Pine Jr. He had on a white suit and a white Gretch guitar case was beside him. He had black, wavy hair and looked like a cross between Tony Curtis and Sal Mineo. I had on a

Ray, "Winnipeg's Elvis"

Woolworth's cowboy shirt, black pants that were shiny from being pressed too much, shoes that were pointed and curled up at the toes. I played a Harmony guitar that my Uncle Sammy bought for me. Needless to say, I felt like the table was parallel with my eyes.

Much to my delight, Pine said he enjoyed my impersonation of Elvis and would I be interested in joining his traveling radio show? I would be paid $15 a night, get to sing a song on every radio program and room with Lenny on the road. I couldn't believe what I was hearing. I said, "Yes! Yes! Yes! When do I start?" He said, "Right away." Lenny then asked if he could play with the band for the rest of the night so he could learn my songs. I was on cloud nine, as we used to say back then.

When Lenny got up on the stage and opened his guitar case, the crowd started to applaud and girls began to scream. He asked if we knew "Freight Train" and started to play it Chet Atkins' style. He brought the house down! The crowd yelled for more and he obliged. I didn't get to sing much that night as they kept wanting more and more of Lenny. The band and I ended up learning *his* tunes that night.

The night was over all too soon for everyone. Pine had left and our steel player, Corky, had his dad's car to give us a ride home. We went to the Salisbury House for something to eat and talked and laughed into the wee hours of the morning.

When Corky dropped me off at home reality kicked in. How was I going to tell Mom and Dad? I was ecstatic about what had happened, but I was just sixteen and was going to have to quit school. It was already Sunday and everyone was home, including Dad! I had to start with Pine on Monday. That fainting feeling was starting all over again.

Much to my surprise, Dad didn't say much, but then he never did unless he had a few beers and started talking politics. I also knew he was very proud of me but didn't want to show it. Mom, on the other hand, was ecstatic that her son was going to be on the radio with stars from "the States." Her biggest worry was how I was going to have clean laundry when I had to travel so much. I told her not to worry; I would be home every Sunday and bring it with me.

Ray – 1956

On Monday morning I showed up at CKY radio studios on Main Street with my new Martin D18 guitar, a pair of white bucks (shoes) and some clothes. We quickly ran over some Elvis songs and got ready to record live to tape. The band consisted of Lenny on his Chet Atkins' orange Gretch guitar played through a Fender Twin amplifier, Jimmy Daughtry on stand-up bass, Betty Cody on vocals, and I played rhythm guitar. We didn't have a drummer because Pine believed everyone on the stage should be a musician. (I'm kidding!!) No, Pine believed that playing CHOP rhythm on the guitar was good enough and in some cases it was. Trying to sing an Elvis tune such as

"Hound Dog" was a little difficult though. Everyone sang at least one song while Pine and Betty carried the entire show. And what show people they were!

In those days, the recording engineer had to have an incredible ear in order to get a good balance. We were fortunate to have Andy Melowanchuck as the engineer. I had been in the studio with Andy a year before singing live on the *Porky Charbbaneau Show*. Here's how we recorded live to tape; singer closest to the microphone, then arrange instruments as to loudness around the microphone. Andy would tell us where to stand until the sound was right.

1957 – Hal Lone Pine, Bev Monroe and Ray St. Germain

Lenny became a master at turning down his guitar.

We would record five, thirty-minute shows, which would be played every morning, Monday to Friday at 7:30 A.M. Then we would hit the road and perform a show in a small town every night except Sunday and Monday. We would appear in theatres and community halls. On Fridays and Saturdays we would also play a three-hour dance in addition to the regular two-hour show.

1959 – Hal Lone Pine Show
Ray doing Elvis

"Colony Street"
Ray with Lenny Breau
Ray snuck out his mom and
dad's car, shut-off the lights
and motor to return it to the
driveway. Couldn't find the
brakes and rolled right into
the house, waking up mom
and dad! Oh, Oh!

Home-on-the-road consisted of country hotels that had the bathroom down the hall with running water, a basin in your room with a pitcher of water, an overhead light bulb hanging down on a wire that you turned on and off with a little chain, and a saggy bed that consisted of a thin mattress thrown over a flat spring holding together the front and back of the bed. Most also had a chest of drawers with a mirror on it.

Lenny and I used to play pool at the Orpheum on Fort Street whenever we were back in town, or any pool hall on the road. On one occasion we were late arriving at the CKY studios where Pine was waiting for us with his Cadillac to drive to our next show out of town.

Pine waited until we got there and fired us on the spot. I guess we forgot the time and I learned another lesson about show business. That's why even today I am always early for a gig or airline flight. But fire your own son? He hired him back and I headed for Dauphin to join the *CKDM Country Kings*. Albert Shorting was on lead guitar, Lou Giroux on Steel and Smokey Chartier on stand up bass. We lived in the Kings Hotel until we were kicked out because we couldn't pay the rent. I didn't know what starving was until I joined the group. We would sometimes finish a dance and drive to the next town and sleep in the car until the town woke up. I gather you know by now we didn't draw many people to our dances. Still, it was an experience I wouldn't trade for anything. Well, other than the people I met, I *would* trade.

10

*1960 – Lenny Breau, Uncle Joe,
Ray St. Germain and Uncle Urban*

1968 – Eaton's fashion show

Ray – 1968

*(Left to Right) Ray, 14 years old,
Alan King's mom and Ray's friend
Alan King*

Chapter 4
Television

My first television appearance was a cross-Canada singing competition called *Talent Caravan* on CBC in 1958. It was the *Canadian Idol* of its day, except the winner was decided by mailing in votes from across Canada. George Murray hosted the show. Although I was making a living on the road with the *Hal Lone Pine Show* and really didn't want to compete in another contest, I did that all my life up until then. Hal Lone Pine encouraged me to enter, telling me this could be a big break for me. A BIG BREAK FOR ME! I thought it already happened. I had shared the stage with this recording star from the United States. I was part of his show. We opened for the traveling stars from the Grand Ole Opry! This included such stars as Johnny Cash, George Jones, Johnny Horton, Porter Wagner, Skeeter Davis and many others.

1957- Porter Wagner

1957
"The Tennessee Two"
Johnny Cash's Band
Marshall Grant and
Luther Perkins

Sisters, a very popular act that drew crowds everywhere. Peggy Neville went on to CBC television fame with "Red River Jamboree" and her own show "The Peggy Neville Show". Barbara Neville was later to become my

wife. The other acts I can't recall.

Much to my surprise, I won. They called my mom and said I had to be in Ottawa the next week to appear on the show as the Winnipeg winner. I was on the road with the Hall Lone Pine Show playing a show in Killarney when they called. I had to leave the next day, but how? I had no way of getting back to Winnipeg to catch the plane. Pine couldn't drive me because he had a show the next day. So I hitchhiked to Winnipeg. I arrived in Ottawa and performed on the show. I also got to play a gig with Ward Allen, a fiddle recording star (he wrote Maple Sugar) and Bob King, a recording star. They asked me to sing with them because they knew Hal Lone Pine.

1957 - Johnny Cash

1957 - Johnny Horton

I decided to enter and got on the show. The show was live from the Playhouse Theatre in Winnipeg. I sang a Billy Grammar song called "Gotta Travel On". I was the only country singer on the show. I didn't think I had a chance. There was a jazz singer, Aubrey Tadman (who later went on to become a television writer and producer in Toronto and Los Angeles), an opera singer, and the Neville

After the performance, I flew back to Winnipeg and rejoined Pine. Later I returned for the semi-finals, also held in Ottawa, but I lost there.

The producer of *Talent Caravan,* Drew Crossman, told me I should move to Toronto if I ever wanted to further my career because that's where everything was happening in the world of show business.

By the way, people who remember *Talent Caravan* confuse me with a fellow who froze on the show and walked off and was called back on stage by George Murray to finish his song. That show was the week before Winnipeg and happened in Vancouver, but it wasn't me.

Chapter 5
Toronto 1959

I was starting to date my future wife, Barbara Neville, when I was in Dauphin, Manitoba. By the time I got back from Dauphin, I only stayed a few months, I played gigs wherever I could in Winnipeg.

While I was in Dauphin, I wrote a couple of songs called "If You Don't Mean It" and "She's a Square". I recorded them at the CKY studios in Winnipeg with Lenny Breau on guitar, Shadow Saunders on stand-up bass, Reg Kelln on drums and a singing group called *The Satins*. (Actually they were called *The Swingtones* when they performed their own shows.) Ted Boittioux, Ron "Rat" Brown and Bill Perry were their names. (I hope I spelled their names correctly.) Andy Melownchuk was the engineer; Alex Groshak produced the session and got the 45-RPM pressed. It was released on Chateau Records out of Toronto and was the first 45 RPM rock & roll record produced in Winnipeg that hit the national charts. It went as high as #7 on most radio stations across Canada.

So, with a hit record under my belt, winning the *Cross-Canada Talent Caravan* TV show in Winnipeg and playing with the Hal Lone Pine Show. I decided to take the plunge and go to Toronto whatever way I could. A disc jockey from CKY Radio called Brian Skinner, "The Chinner Spinner", told me he was moving to Toronto to join a radio station there and I could get a ride with him. He was leaving within the week.

What a break! Toronto was waiting for me and I was coming! I was going to set that town on its ear. I was finally going to hit the big time! Grab the brass ring! It was happening!

But what was I going to tell Barbara? I told her there was only room for me in the car, but when I got there I would find a place and send for her. She said her parents would never go for that. So, I suggested we elope. We were both nineteen and knew everything. Besides, when they found out, I would be on my way to being a star. So we eloped on October 7th, 1959. Then Barbara went home to her parents and I went home to pack. Lenny Breau had married my sister Val two weeks before, only Val had invited our parents to the wedding.

I arrived in Toronto thinking, 'Wait until the agents find out I'm here; they will be so impressed.' Not! When I arrived in Toronto with Brian Skinner he asked where I was going to stay. I hadn't thought about that. He dropped me off at the YMCA near College and Yonge. I got a room, with the little money I had, and was set to conquer Toronto, the Centre of the Universe. I called the producer of *Talent Caravan* and said, "Here I am, now what?" He told me to contact the Billy O'Conner booking agency. I thought this was the greatest. He would make me a star! Billy said he would see me and talk about some shows he had on the go. I walked to his office about ten blocks away and sat in the reception area waiting. He was busy with other acts and his secretary asked me to come back in about a week. This waiting went on for a while.

I finally found a third floor walk-up near College and Spadina where the rent was cheap. My money was getting low and I had to call Mom and Dad for a loan. I hated to do that because I had told them I was becoming a star in T.O. On top of that, my wife, Barbara, had just told me she was pregnant (with our first daughter, Chrystal) and was wondering when she could come to Toronto. I told her everything was going great and I would send for her as soon as I rented a super apartment.

Back and forth to Billy's office I went-still no jobs. I finally went to Chateau Records which was owned by Art Snider. He told me that since my songs were not published, I should meet the young man who ran his publishing company, Ardo Music, and publish my songs. I met the young man who was a dancer with the Swinging Singing Eight on the CBC show called *Country Hoedown* hosted by Gordie Tapp. That man was Gordon Lightfoot, a clean cut, young songwriter who somehow knew my situation; I was a stranger, not from T.O. I'll never forget his kindness.

On one trip to O'Conner's office I met a young Joey Hollingsworth while we were both waiting in Billy's office. Joey was already an established entertainer. He could dance, he could sing and was a quality performer. Everybody knew Joey! He told me Billy had so many performers to book and sometimes had difficulty placing them all. My time would come he assured me. Joey gave me a ride home that day in his Cadillac and we became life-long friends.

Joey was promoting a new record and was to do a television show in North Bay, Ontario. He told me he had convinced the producers to also put me on the show to promote my record. He picked me up and we drove to North Bay. He even paid me to perform out of his own pocket. I refused the money, but he insisted. I took it because I had to pay the rent.

Then Billy called me and said he had a way for me to make some money. I thought, 'Finally, a chance to show Toronto what this country boy can do.' When I arrived at the office, he asked me if I knew anything about cars. CARS! I knew how to put gas in them and check the oil. That was it! He said his brother was the general manager of a car dealership called Levin's Motors and they needed a control operator. I had no idea what

he was talking about but I said, "Oh yeah, I know a lot about cars." I was on the verge of starving and had to survive somehow. So, I went to see about the job and I got it. I lied through my teeth. The control operator sat in the tower and distributed the jobs to the mechanics. You had to know what each mechanic specialized in. The fellow who was leaving trained me and probably laughed all the way home that night and thought what a way to get even with the dealership.

I had made friends with a mechanic called Ray Bruce who helped me through this harrowing experience. He knew my situation and I repaid him by giving him most of the jobs. Mechanics made a percentage on all the work they did.

In the meantime, I had to figure a way to bring Barbara to Toronto. I still wasn't making enough money to afford what I said I could. I thought my singing career was done as far as Toronto was concerned. So, I pawned my Martin D18 that I bought while I was with Hal Lone Pine and bought Barbara the plane ticket. Ray Bruce drove me to the airport to pick her up. As we drove back to the third- floor walk-up single room suite I was staying in I was trying to figure a way to tell her I had failed. Fortunately, she understood and we lived there until we couldn't take it anymore, and decided to return to Winnipeg.

I bought a 1954 Pontiac that Ray Bruce had worked on. He told me not to drive it over 50 miles per hour on the way back to Winnipeg. It was a long drive back and when we arrived we stayed with her parents.

I was feeling like a complete loser. I called Hal Lone Pine who was now in Moose Jaw, Saskatchewan doing a radio show at CHAB Radio and touring. His son, my best friend and now brother-in-law, Lenny Breau, was still with him. Pine told me I had the job so I left the next day leaving Barabara and our daughter, Chrystal, with her parents.

In Moose Jaw, I stayed in the Harwood Hotel and roomed with Lenny again. Guitar players to this day ask me if Lenny gave me lessons because we stayed together so much. The answer is yes, he tried, but I was more interested in singing. Besides, I would never be as good as Lenny on guitar and always be a poor imitation. You have to know the pure talent he had and the dedication that I've never witnessed again to this day.

It was now 1960 and Lenny and I would talk for hours on end, when he wasn't practicing, about what we were going to do with the rest of our lives. Lenny wanted to play jazz and take guitar where it had never been. We both realized we were too young to be fathers, but we were. I had my daughter Chrystal and he had a daughter named Melody, my niece. I wanted to be the next Elvis. What were we both doing in Moose Jaw? There was nothing wrong with Moose Jaw, but it was a long way from L.A. and Memphis.

Things started to change. I moved Barbara and Chrystal to Moose Jaw and we stayed in a basement suite. One night, during a show Lenny played a jazz solo on one of the songs his dad was singing, a song called "O Lonesome Me" written by Don Gibson. Pine slapped him across the face during intermission and told him never to do that again. It was the slap that changed the jazz world. Lenny quit and went back to Winnipeg to play with the jazz players he loved-Bob Erlandson, Ronnie Halldorson, Reg Kelln, Dave Shaw, Dave Young, Gary Gross, many more and his favorite singer, Mary Nelson.

I stayed in Moose Jaw with the Pine Show until Hal suddenly left one night back to Bangor, Maine. He still had bookings that had to be filled. Jack Paget, bass and steel guitar plus singer, and comedian Uncle Hiram who played the banjo, asked if Barbara would fill in and she did. We filled the dates and moved back to Winnipeg.

Once again, we stayed at her parents' place. Her father, Arnold Neville, God bless his soul, somehow still believed in me-probably thinking, 'God, please help this poor idiot provide a home for my daughter and my grandchild.' I'm pretty sure her mother, Theresa, thought that every day.

He finally said to me that maybe this career of mine wasn't going too well, that maybe I should consider a day job. By this time, Barbara was pregnant with our daughter Cathy.

His neighbor worked at McCabe Grain, in the Grain Exchange, as an executive and said he could get me a job. I started working in the mailroom delivering mail. I couldn't believe my singing career was pretty much over. I was a father that actually had a day job and had to become responsible. I took the bus to work, brought my lunch, and wore a Fedora. We had now bought a little house at 116 Berrydale in St. Vital and I had a 1949 Desoto. I grew a moustache and goatee, had two beautiful daughters and a loving wife. I was actually thinking of building a white picket fence. I was becoming one of them! I worked there from 1960 to 1965. Eventually I was promoted to the sample room grading grain.

Chapter 6
More Television

One day, in 1963, I was called by a producer, Ray McConnell, at the CBC in Winnipeg, to audition for a new Big Band show they were going to produce called *Like Young*.

By this time I was doing some gigs on weekends with Lenny Breau. We called ourselves the *Mississippi Gamblers* and played the Showboat Drive-in on North Main in Winnipeg, and I still worked at the Grain Exchange. Len Andree, a comedian and booking agent, also used me on gigs and I even played straight man to his gags.

The audition turned into an interview because he already knew my work and was a Lenny Breau fan. Bob McMullin was the band leader and some of the best musicians in Winnipeg were in the band including Lenny. I sang the Big Band songs of the day and hosted the show. It was a 13-week gig broadcast locally once a week.

This led to me being the singing host of a new national series called *Music Hop Hootenanny*. It started in 1964 and went on until 1966, 39 half-hour shows a year, seen at 5:30 PM Monday to Friday, coast to coast in Canada on the CBC network. The other *Music Hops* came from Halifax, Montreal (Pierre LaLonde) Toronto (Alex Trebeck)-yes, that Alex Trebeck (*Jeopardy*)-and Vancouver (Terry David Mulligan). The *Winnipeg Music Hop* was seen on Wednesdays.

Once again Bob McMullin wrote all the arrangements and Ray McConnell produced the show. When the show began the cast consisted of: Band – Lenny Breau, (guitar) – Wayne Finucan, (drums) and Dave Young, (bass) who later went on to become one of the best jazz bassist in the country. Chorus and featured

1964 – CBC Ray St. Germain
Music Hop Hootennay

performers were: Yvette Shaw (still one of my favorite singers who went on to host her own television series), Mickey Allen, Carol West, 14-year-old Lucille Emond, Sam McConnell Jr., Hector Bremnar and Barry Stillwell, who went on to musical theatre. We sang rock & roll, folk songs and even a little country. Chad Allen joined the chorus in 1966 and the next year when Music Hop was cancelled, Chad hosted a series in the same time slot with The Guess Who called "Let's Go".

McCabe Grain gave me an ultimatum in 1965 to make up my mind about which career I wanted to pursue: be a grain inspector or a television performer. Duh! I was making enough money between CBC and playing gigs around town booked by Len Andree that the grain business was slowing my comeback in the business that I loved. I thought I could make enough now

L-R: Ray St. Germaine, Wayne Finucan, Kaz Sivell.
Eaton's fashion show. Winnipeg, 1965.
Owen Clark Collection. Photo contributed by Lillian Vadeboncoeur. Photo ID: OC-201.

that I wasn't burdened with a day job. I even bought a brand new 1966 Dodge Coronet Convertible. As soon as I did that, *Music Hop* was cancelled. Oh, Oh! Now I had to get more work to make up for the *Music Hop* wages I lost.

CBC producers were good to me though. They booked me on other variety shows as a guest. One of the shows I was hoping to host was *Hymn Sing* that went on for something like thirty years. After all, it started because in 1965 during the *Music Hop* series we were asked to do a Good Friday *Music Hop* special in place of the Friday Halifax show. As a chorus, only a few of us were good sight (music note) readers. I wasn't one of them. The show got a ton of mail and phone calls. It was a hit. People liked the idea of young people singing hymns on television. The CBC decided to create *Hymn Sing*. I asked if I could host the new series but was told I already was the host of *Music Hop* and it would be a conflict.

However, they hired one of our cast members, Barry Stillwell, as one of their early hosts. Maybe I didn't get it because I wasn't a good sight reader or because I played bars-not a good image.

I continued to play lounges and bars around town along with guesting on CBC shows. CBC producers in Toronto started to book me as a guest host on several TV specials. *Show of the Week* and *In Person* were just a few that I remember. My guests included Ian and Sylvia Tyson, Gordon Lightfoot, Anne Murray and a host of others that were stars in Canada.

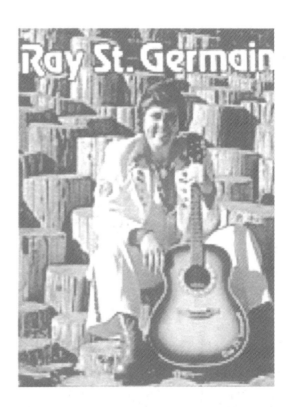

Chapter 7
Chan's Moon Room Cabaret

One of the first nightclubs I ever played, early in my career, was Chan's Moon Room. It was located on Main Street about a block north of Portage Avenue in downtown Winnipeg. The building was three stories high. On the first floor they had Chan's Restaurant. The second boasted a dining room and lounge and on the third, Chan's Moon Room Cabaret, dancing and entertainment until 2 A.M., six nights a week.

The room was one of the best nightclubs in the '50's and '60's. It featured acts from the U.S.A. and across Canada. *The Bernie Shaw Trio* with Moose Jackson on bass, Del Wagner on drums and Bernie on piano, backed the acts and played dance music.

When the club decided to change the format and book self-contained local acts, we were one of the first acts to play the room. We were booked in the room by Len Andree of Andree Productions Ltd for a period of three weeks in the beginning of 1967. We, meaning Kas Siwik on electrovox (an accordion that played like an organ on the key side and bass on the button side), Wayne Finucan on drums, and me on guitar and lead vocals, did so well in the room we were asked to stay for the remainder of year and the following two years.

Four Chinese men owned the whole operation. One of the owners and the man who was in charge of everything was Charlie Foo, a man in his 80's who was affectionately called "Mayor of Chinatown". Charlie had an accent when he talked and when people would comment on how well he spoke English, he would smile and say with his Chinese accent, "Of course you damn-a-fool. I born here!" No one knew when Charlie came to Canada or how.

It didn't matter; he was a remarkable man and quite a character.

Charlie's office was located on the second floor right below the dance floor. Now Charlie was used to hearing the soft shuffling of dance feet above him as previous bands played soft jazz and standards. We had been there a month when our pro-country crowd started to find us and yell for dances that had never been played in this night club. One night, at about 11 P.M. they demanded the dreaded polka. At the same time, every night at 11 P.M., the waitress brought Charlie his consommé soup and grilled sandwich to his office underneath the dance floor. Just as he was about to eat, we started playing a polka and the crowd packed the dance floor kickin' and stompin'. At the same time, a huge chunk of plaster from the ceiling came loose and fell in his bowl, splashing soup all over his suit. We were still playing the polka when through the crowd came Charlie Foo waving his serviette and yelling "Stop a – da music. Stop a – da music." We quit playing and everyone stopped dancing. Then Charlie got on the stage, grabbed the microphone and scolded the crowd and the band. "What's a da matta with you damn-a-fool? You jump up and a-down the whole building fall in." I heard a female voice in the crowd say "Oh, my God." Charlie then turned to me and said, "If you ever play the damn-a-fool music again, you fired."

Now, not knowing what really happened to cause that stain on the front of his pants, I figured he got scared and he peed himself. I took the microphone and said, "Mr. Foo. On behalf of the audience and the band, I apologize for frightening you so much." The audience burst out laughing, the band nearly peed themselves from laughing. Then the thought of getting fired struck me right then and there, so I kept a straight face while I shook Mr. Foo's hand. He quickly left the stage and never mentioned the incident again. Of course, we never played a polka there again.

Right across from Charlie's office door on the second floor stood the lounge bar. Right behind the bar stood the bartender in full view of Mr. Foo. Without actually asking the bartender, Charlie was trying to figure out how the bartender got so drunk on one drink at the end of the night. Charlie started asking the staff and the band if they knew how he was doing it. One of the staff members tipped the bartender off and got the whole story. He had the vodka behind the bar out of sight, placed with the other bottles near the sink, also out of the view of Charlie Foo. Whenever he wanted a drink he'd run the tap water and reach for a water tumbler. He would fill the tumbler with vodka, turn off the water, salute Mr. Foo and and down the vodka!

By the way, it was the bartender who told us what happened to Charlie when the ceiling fell in his soup. He said he laughed so hard he almost dropped the vodka bottle.

As I mentioned, Chan's had three floors. To get to the Moon Room Cabaret on the third floor, you could walk up the stairs or take the "famous-for-getting-stuck-between- floors" elevator. When the bar closed at two in the morning, most people took their chances with the stairs.

The building next to Chan's housed the studios of CKY Radio. The disc jockeys would put on a long-playing record, climb on the roof of the CKY building, down the fire escape to the alley below, and into the back door of Chan's main floor. Up the back stairs of Chan's they would go, through the second floor kitchen and up to the Moon Room where they would emerge from behind the stage and walk calmly up to the bar and order a drink. They would down the drink, walk back past the band grinning like a Cheshire cat, and quickly negotiate the obstacle course back to the control room where they always seemed to arrive just in time for the song to end.

Back to the "famous-for-getting-stuck-between- floors" elevator. One afternoon I was in the Moon Room setting up some equipment when I heard the elevator again. I figured someone from one of the other floors would call the elevator people and calm down the poor unfortunate soul. The bell kept ringing and I realized that everyone in the building was thinking the same thing. I ran over to the elevator door and yelled down the shaft, "Who's down there?" Charlie Foo's voice shot back, "What the hell it matter who down here? Someone important or not important. Still stuck you damn-a-fool." I suppressed my laughter and told him I would get help. Soon after, the elevator started to move and Charlie got off, yelling that he was going to sue the elevator company. Now he knew how hundreds of other people felt.

One night the Moon Room was really slow. Our new singer with the band, Sherisse, had just joined us and was singing on stage with the boys. I was standing at the back of the room checking out the sound when Charlie came up behind me and said, "You told me would be good for business. There no one-a-here." I answered back, "Mr. Foo, Sherisse just started tonight. We haven't advertised her yet. Besides, the Blue Bombers are playing tonight at Winnipeg Stadium." Charlie smiled that sarcastic smile when he though you just said something really stupid. "Oh, I didn't know the stadium held 500,000 a people!" The stadium held at the time only 20,000 and the population of Winnipeg was 500,000. Got me again!

Before Sherisse joined the band, we had to back up a few acts that Charlie would book every now and then. We had some singers, strippers, fire baton acts, magicians etc. etc. One week he booked a three hundred pound stripper and her singing Chihuahua. She did three shows a night. Her act consisted of singing a few songs and stripping. You should have seen the view from behind. And I mean BEHIND! On her final number she would bring out her little dog. I think she would hide it under one of her folds. She would stand there, singing naked, except for two tassels on her breasts and a G-string, holding the dog in her hand. The dog would always howl right on cue. I thought, 'What a talented little dog'. The audience thought so too. One night I saw how she got the dog to howl at the right time.

She would stick her pinky finger up the dog's rear end. I thought I was going to be sick. What a dog act. But the Chihuahua was cute.

1957 – The *Hal Lone Pine Show*

Chapter 8
Northern Manitoba Tours

In 1967, it was Canada's 100th Birthday and celebrations were taking place all over the country. I was asked by the Manitoba Government to take a show to Northern Manitoba and celebrate with remote northern communities. We would visit thirty four communities in twenty one days on single engine Otter float planes. This included Kas Siwik on accordian, Wayne Finucan on drums and me on acoustic guitar, plus singing and MCing the shows. We also had a magician by the name of Ray Starr.

1967 Northern Tour – Ray Starr - Magician

The rest of the show was made up of talent show winners held in Thompson. I had never been north of Dauphin. Neither had Kas, Wayne or Ray Starr. It was an adventure we'll never forget. The talent plus the northern coordinator, John McDonald who was also a deputy minister, flew on one of the Otters. The luggage and equipment flew on the other. We also had a Beaver aircraft as a runner back and forth to Thompson to get needed supplies such as huge Centennial Birthday Cakes.

We were based out of Thompson but stayed wherever we could because most of the time we had to perform in two communities a day. We had a small battery-operated PA system with one microphone because we never knew if we would be performing in the band hall, a make-shift stage or on a flat piece of ground. It was really remote as there was no road access and very few landing strips. The people spoke their language, Cree or Ojibway, and not many spoke English. John McDonald was a great help because he could understand the language of the communities.

We would land on the water and carry our equipment up the bank to wherever we would do the show. The people would help us and made us feel very welcome. We would meet the chief and council and elders and do the show. The communities were presented with a Centennial Cake and flag.

Someone in the government at the time insisted we close the show with the song "This Land is Your Land. This Land is My Land". I said no, I wouldn't be singing that song. Nora McLeod, a jigger from Cross Lake and I used to sing different words and laugh on the plane. "This land is my land, This land is my land, it's not your land anymore." Sad but true.

Three years later, in 1970, it was Manitoba's Centennial and I was then again asked to bring a show to the North with the same format. We did and that's when I met Ernest Monais, whose brother, William, was on the show in 1967, along with Nikko Ross (fantastic fiddle player). Again, we traveled by the dreaded single engine Otters but flown by outstanding pilots-Merv Zikman, Connie Lamb, Ray Mason and others I can't remember.

I may be mixing up the performers and pilots because it was so long ago and the tours were close together but the experience was the same. I met some outstanding people up north and I have great respect for them all. One fellow I got to meet was Luke Harper from Garden Hill and his family. We still keep in touch. His wife still makes the best bread in Canada and Luke still tells the best jokes I've ever heard.

One of the shows was in Ilford. When we landed, we were told they would like to have a parade. What! A Parade? The community had a street only four blocks long or so. We agreed and Wayne Finucan, strapped his bass drum on with a rope and Kas Siwik played his accordian and Sandy played his bagpipes while we marched down the street, with the whole community in the parade. No one watched except a dog wagging his tail.

We played a show in Thicket Portage on the hottest day of the summer. We had set up on the shore and were sweating during the performance. I asked for some water to drink and someone brought a pail and a dipper for us to drink. The water was so cool and refreshing we drank the whole pail. It was pure lake water, something our bodies were not used to. We flew back to Thompson that evening and became very ill. Wayne, Kas and I spent the night taking turns in the bathroom and shaking. A doctor finally arrived and gave us a shot of something to calm us down. We had to cancel the next day to recover and made up the shows by doing three a day. Hank Light was also a tour coordinator in the 1970 tour. He was an ex

RCMP Officer and how he put up with us is probably something he still talks about. Hank was a perfect gentleman.

Another time we played Norway House the same time Prince Charles was to visit. They had an outdoor stage built with entertainment from the community to perform for the Prince.

We were told not to set up any equipment on the stage until after Prince Charles had left. They had a beaded cushion for him to sit on while he was entertained. Our Scotsman, Sandy, did not like royalty and let us know. After the Prince left, the cushion disappeared and we were the suspects. When we asked Sandy if he had taken the cushion, he assured us he wouldn't touch anything that Prince Charles had passed wind on. The cushion finally turned up and we went on with the show. When the Prince left on his military helicopter they had trouble and had to land while the backup helicopter picked him up and continued on. I kept thinking, "I hope they don't think we had anything to do with that."

Chapter 9
My Journals

In 1967, I kept a journal of our Northern tour and had misplaced it for many years. While writing this book I finally came across it. Some of the pages were water stained and I couldn't make out a lot of what I had written down. But, here it is:

July 2nd – flew to Thompson from Winnipeg and saw first forest fire near Thicket Portage. Mary Liz Bayer from the Manitoba Government, Ray Starr, Hugh Penwarden in charge of monkey and lovebirds join me there.

July 3rd – Thompson to Thicket Portage-Outdoor show about 250 people – Hugh Penwarden dresses as clown and hands out balloons, sparklers and birthday cake. Monkey steals show. Fly back to Thompson.

July 4th – Thompson to Split Lake – Show at 11:00 AM – Merv Zikman wears clown suit – Darn monkey steals show again. Fly to Ilford – Show inside hall at 8:00 PM – 150 people. Nikko and William play dance after. Tribute to pioneers Oliver and Julie Lindal. Saw my first "Smiling Johnny" poster-advertising dance next night. Stayed overnight.

July 5th – Gillam – shows at 3:00 PM and 8:00 PM – Merv Zikman didn't like strong crosswind and wouldn't take chance landing on river. He had all the talent on board. So he told me he was going to land on a tiny little lake that looked like a pond. He skimmed the shore, landed and stopped just about at the end of the other shore. When I stopped shaking I said, "Okay Batman, how are we going to take off?" He said, "Not we. I will take off now and land on the river and meet everybody there." And he did. What a fantastic pilot he was. This time Nora Mcleod steals the show. Locked up monkey. Stayed in bunkhouses overnight.

July 6th – Left for Churchill – See fewer and fewer trees until flat barren land with pools of water with ice lining the shores. I was told to look for rocks under the water as Merv made a pass over where he wanted to land the plane. Oh, my God! Me? I'm responsible for a safe landing? He told me not to worry, as he would be looking too. We landed and as we were heading for the dock the plane lurched to the left. Of course, my side of the plane. We either hit a rock or Merv did it on purpose because he was laughing his head off at my reaction. Stayed at Hudson Hotel and did show in the hall. Nora McLeod's birthday. Saw Elsie and Tom Christianson, friends of my mom and dad.

July 7th – Left Churchill for Shamattawa – saw rusted ship that hit a sandbar twenty years before and split in two – also see abandoned Fort York – Do show and stay overnight.

July 8th – God's Lake Narrows – (If I don't mention anything about some communities, it's because I couldn't read the water stained pages). Do show and leave for Garden Hill – Merv Zikman leaves us today. A new pilot by the name of Frank Hanson joins us. He was a WWII flying ace and loved to beat the other planes in for a landing. These pilots are simply amazing! Leave for St. Theresa Point and stay with priest. Show at 8:30 PM.

July 9th – Oxford House. Very beautiful. Met Minister Ian Harland and his wife, Donna, also Chief Thomas, a very smart man. The government wants to build an airstrip using workers from elsewhere and bulldozers to clear the land. Chief Thomas wants his community to have the work instead. He has a lot of other ideas for Oxford House. I hope he gets his way. Left for Thompson, stayed at Burntwood Motel – washed clothes and had my own room. (Good friend, Sheila North, NCI broadcaster is from

Oxford House. She wasn't born when I was there).

July 10th – Leave Thompson for Cross Lake. Show at 11:00 AM in hall – Nikko went home for a couple of hours. The Chief had on a black suit with red stripes on pants, yellow piping on collar and cuffs. Travel by boat to Norway House and stay at Playgreen Inn. The weather is getting bad and got soaked in boat. Hope guitar is not wet. Show at 8:00 PM. See another "Smiling Johnny" poster. I think he is following us. Yeah, but he doesn't have a monkey.

July 11th – Still in Norway House because weather has us socked in. A bad storm. Have to cancel Poplar River and Berens River. We'll try to make up shows at some point. Pilots ready to fly but Hank says no. I get to meet Joe Keeper, 1912 Olympic Champion. (I now know he is the grandfather of actress Tina Keeper and Joy Keeper, good friends of mine.)

July 12th – Left for Grand Rapids. Show at 9:00 PM. Stayed at LaSalle Motel, owner Mr. Pouliet, met Joe Geonett. Had trip to power plant.

July 13th – Easterville. Show at 1:30 PM. Met Chester Beaven. Frank Hanson leaves and another pilot joins us by the name of Gerry Mason. (Good friend Lorraine George, former NCI broadcaster, is from Easterville and tells me she was only one year old when I was there. I told her I remembered her.

Leave Moose Lake. Show outside around 6:00 PM. Stayed with Connie Lamb's sister and husband, Jock McAree. They own Lamb's store, very hospitable people. Have moose meat and moose heart. Connie tells me of caves there with very old drawings on walls. Wish we had time to see that.

July 14th – Cormorant. Show at 11:00 AM. Stage against lake, very beautiful. Connie hates monkey as it bites him at every chance. Connie said if he had to unload the monkey one more

time and it bites him, he will drop the monkey and cage in the lake. A fellow by the name of Bill Ducharme jigs with Nora McLeod. John McDonald with his wife and child join us flying in on Beaver aircraft.

Leave for Snow Lake. Check into hotel owned by Adam Bud and his wife who used to own Lincoln Hotel in Winnipeg. Show at 8:00 PM in hall. Jo-Anne and Hugh not talking. Anne Ridgeway leaves show for Montreal with her husband. Hotel has television and direct telephone line to Winnipeg.

July 15th and 16th – Sheridan. Show at 3:00 PM. Stayed at Cambrian Hotel owned by Walter Shmon. He reads us poetry. Have a pitcher of water in each room. Hot water in hallway heated by an old washing machine. Cold water from rain barrel on roof. Walter opens beer parlour for us and plays us old '78 records. The town is pretty much deserted as copper mine had closed. Walter still has claims for land and hopes they will re-open. Walter takes us fishing and I caught so many jackfish. I threw back about five. Walter gives me Master Angler lighter. That night he gives us Grandpa's stuff and we end up walking around the edge of the roof trying to balance our way without falling off. It must have been good stuff because we didn't fall.

July 17th – Pukatawagon. Show at 1:00 PM. Outside. Hottest day yet. Still feeling Grandpa's stuff. MP Bud Simpson joins us for remainder of trip. Connie brings his wife, Nancy. Still threatens to drop monkey in lake. He suggests since monkey always-stealing show, to celebrate Canada's Centennial year, we put a Canadian flag in each of his hands. Stick a sparkler up its behind and whiz him across the stage.

Leave for Granville Lake. Outside show at 5:00 PM. Population seventy-two. Colourful cabins. Not many speak English so my impersonations of singers don't go over too well. Damn monkey steals show again. I'm starting to agree with Connie.

Leave for Lynn Lake. Check into Hotel. Connie Lamb left today for Arctic. Bob Shinny takes over. We will miss Connie and his on going feud with the monkey. The monkey was holding his head and couldn't stand up in his cage like he was drunk when Connie left. We suspect that Connie got his revenge by having a drink with him.

July 18th – Brochet. Show at 12:00 PM. About five-hundred people. John McDonald and wife join us. People came in yesterday for show and pitched tents. Told it's the coldest place in Manitoba. Raining now and had to cut the show short. Must remember Thomson Highway, good looking Chippewayan kid, 18, who plays classical piano taught by the nuns here. They use dog teams here and put the dogs on an island and throw fish to them to eat. They're too wild for the community. Left Brochet at 3:00 PM in driving rain. Oh Lord, please be with us.

Arrive Lynn Lake at 4:30 PM. Show at 8:00 PM in hall. About five-hundred people. Meet big folk singer by the name of Jumbo. Stay at Fairview Hotel. Pilot Bob Shinny is clown today. Hugh taken to hospital because of nerves. We all felt like joining him. Gwen Johnson leaves show today for Morris, Manitoba.

July 19th – Nelson House. Left Thompson at 1:30 PM and arrived in Nelson House at 2:00 PM. Show at 3:00 PM. It's too hot even for the monkey. Just finish show and big storm hits. Can't leave until 9:30 PM. Hudson Bay guys give us rum and nursing station gives us supper. Meet Mr. Olson. Arrive Thompson at 10:00 PM and go to party at Don Johnson's home. Back to motel at 2:00 AM.

July 21st – Poplar River. Show at 3:00 PM. One-hundred people. Bought some beadwork. Hudson Bay staff feeds us.

Left for Berens River at 3:30 PM, arrive at 6:00 PM. Show at 9:00 PM outside. Three-hundred people. Met Ma Kemp and son Dick, had party until 2:00 AM. I think monkey still a hit but getting on our nerves. Stayed at RC mission.

July 22nd – Leave Berens at 9:00 AM in Beachcraft. New pilot says he needs flying time. What! I am now going home to Winnipeg. He tells me he never landed on the Red River. From the air it looks like a slithering snake. Please God, let him land this plane on the river. He did and we taxied to Rivercrest - Home at last! I wonder whatever happened to that monkey…

It was an experience I'll never forget and I thank the Lord for keeping us all safe. The bush pilots are the greatest flyers in the world and I would fly with them anywhere. They have a special bond with guardian angels I'm sure.

Chapter 10
Anne Murray and Re-uniting
with Hal Lone Pine

At this time I was living in Winnipeg playing Chan's Moon Room and flying back and forth to Toronto to host CBC Specials and guest on the Tommy Hunter Show.

1968 – CBC, Reg Gibson and Ray St. Germain

Anne Murray was a regular on *Sing-along-Jubilee* from Halifax when she made a guest appearance on "In Person" from Toronto, Studio 4 on Yonge Street in 1968. Her first album had not been released yet. She had been a faithful watcher of *Music Hop* and we hit it off right away. She seemed like a Winnipegger. I was a big fan of hers. We were on set, waiting for lights to be adjusted, when I took my guitar and started playing the intro to "The Ode To Billy-Joe" which wasn't the song she was about to sing but she started singing it. The producer Mark Warren was recording the audio and kept

it just because he said it sounded great. I wish I had that recording now. The producer went on to produce *Sanford & Son* in the USA.

During the same show Anne was rehearsing her song when the studio lights went out. It was break time for the crew and the union was punctual. I walked up to her and explained what had happened and said it was lunch break. I said that I was going for lunch and would she join me. We had lunch and I picked up the tab. She insisted on paying her share, but I told her the next time it would be her treat. I didn't realize it would be one year later before we would work together again and she would be on her way to becoming a star.

That time came in late 1969 when I was co-hosting with Pat Harvey an hour TV special for CBC called *Two for the Road*. Pat and I, with the CBC crew, traveled across Canada from Halifax to Vancouver. The first stop was Halifax. When I arrived at the hotel, I went down for dinner and when I tried to pay the bill, the waiter told me it was picked up by Anne Murray. I then remembered her words in Toronto. What a terrific, wonderful person. No wonder she remains a star.

Anne was one of our guest performers on that special and she had just recorded her first album. Yes, *that* album! The one that would send her on her way to becoming a star, "Snowbird!" After the taping of the show, we all decided to go out and have a few drinks. The *Rhythm Pals* from the *Tommy Hunter Show* were also in town and we hooked up with them. They wanted to go to a lounge where they said someone I knew was playing. I wondered who it was and then they told me. Hal Lone Pine and his new wife, Jeannie, were playing there. HAL

LONE PINE! Lenny Breau's dad, the man who taught me about show business, RCA Victor recording star and former host of the *Louisiana Hayride*. The man who left his own show in Moose Jaw on CHAB and who slapped his son into becoming a Jazz legend.

I was so happy I was going to see him again. We all met there and I was so excited to hear him once again. Jack Jensen of the *Rhythm Pals* turned to me and said, "We are watching a legend of show business." You're telling me? I was the fortunate soul he picked to join his traveling radio show.

Long Pine looked embarrassed when we walked in. It was a small lounge and there weren't many people there. As a matter of fact, I think we doubled the people in the room when we all walked in. There was just the two of them; Hal and Jeannie on bass. He was singing the same songs I remember him singing when we toured and playing that big old Gibson Hummingbird. I just knew he was looking for a way out of the room to avoid me. To tell you the truth, I was embarrassed for him. Is this the way a career in the music business ends, if you don't have hit record after hit record? Do you end up playing small lounges from town to town? Are your car and your clothes the only things you end up with? I was starting to realize the cold hard truth about show business.

Lone Pine finished his set and came over to the table. He still was wearing the rhinestone suit but didn't have on his trademark white cowboy hat. Instead, he had on his head a black curly toupee, a la Tom Jones, that didn't fit too well. He only stayed for a few minutes to say "Hi" and quickly left. I was so hurt that he

didn't congratulate me for my success, which I owed all to him.

I heard later that he died alone in a hotel room after a show in Bangor, Maine. I cried a lot after hearing that. That's one of the stories of show business we don't hear about unless they are currently on the hit parade. Hal Lone Pine was my mentor and the father of one of my best friends, Lenny Breau. He taught me so much about show business just by watching him night after night and seeing how he could entertain and control an audience. Over the years I've had the opportunity to work with many stars, but the greatest entertainer I've ever witnessed on stage was HAL LONE PINE!

Ray and Dave Dudley 'CBC' taping
'My Kind of Country' - 1970

Chapter 11
Back to Toronto

Aubrey Tadman and Gary Ferrier flew in from Toronto to audition me for the host of a new variety television show they were producing out of T.O. called *The 1969 Electric Powered Television Show*. They were auditioning several people throughout Canada and said it would be a Big Band Show with the Rick Wilkins Orchestra featuring members of the award-winning Boss Brass. They knew I had been singing and hosting variety shows in Winnipeg with the Bob McMullin Orchestra on the CBC Network. I thought 'Here is my chance to get back to Toronto.' If only I could pass the audition which took place at the CBC Winnipeg Studios". They had me sing everything from Country to Big Band Swing.

We had just bought a new house in Ft. Garry at 322 Marshall Bay and Barbara was pregnant with our third child, Ray Jr. I remembered how long television variety shows lasted and we were a little worried about what we would do if I got the show. Would we sell the house and move or should I go by myself until I was sure I was firmly established in the centre of the universe?

It wasn't long before I got the call from Toronto saying I was chosen to host the network show. The producer was to be Ray McConnell. I had worked with Ray when he was in Winnipeg producing *Music Hop Hootenanny* so I was excited that we would work together again. He was a very talented producer and a friend. (He went on to produce *Front Page Challenge* for many years.)

Now came the time to make up our minds about the move. The show was sponsored by Texaco and I had a five year contract with one stipulation: The show could be cancelled after thirteen weeks. I would be told after nine weeks if the show would last the year and after that it would be a yearly thing up to five years. I think it was thirty-nine shows a year. What to do? Everyone was excited about the new show in Toronto so we sold the house and rented a U-Haul pulled by my 1966 Dodge Coronet Convertible with pregnant Barbara, nine-year-old Chrystal, seven-year-old Cathy, and me. We sold most of the furniture and just took what we thought we would need to start our new life in Toronto.

We stayed in a three-bedroom apartment in Don Mills, Ontario. Quite a difference from the first time I moved there ten years before and stayed in that one room walk-up on College and Spadina. But I was back and this time I had hold of the brass ring.

I showed up for the first rehearsal at CBC on Jarvis. By this time I knew that the writers for the show had changed. They were now Alan Thicke and Vern Kennedy. (Alan later became a star in the U.S.A.) Norm Amadio was the rehearsal pianist and also part of the Big Band. We taped the first show at Studio 4 on Yonge Street in front of an audience. I sang Frank Sinatra, Jack Jones, etc. with the orchestra. By the way, during rehearsal with the big band, I kept messing up because I kept listening to the marvelous sound they produced. On a break, trumpet player Arnie Chinowski (I hope I spelled his name correctly) told me to not listen too much to the band and concentrate on my vocals because if I keep making mistakes, I wouldn't be here very long, but they would. I took his advice. Another thing I noticed about how great they were is that they would send in sub players for rehearsal and then come in and nail the charts cold for the show. I was definitely movin' on up to the big time. Some of the other names I remember in Rick Wilkinson's band were: Ed Bickard-guitar,

Jerry Fuller-drums, Butch Wattanabe-trombone, Moe Koffman-saxaphone, Guido Basso-trumpet and so many other great musicians that slip my mind now because it was so long ago.

During the taping of the fifth or sixth show, my wife went into labour and was rushed to St. Michael's Hospital by her sister Peggy Neville, who lived in the same apartment block, and called me. She was still in labour and we couldn't stop the show. I rushed to the hospital after the taping and Ray Jr. was born shortly thereafter, on November 6th.

In the meantime, I was featured in a Toronto newspaper, T.V. guide and also gave an interview to a T.V. critic about the show. We met in a coffee shop and he copied down what I was saying. At least I thought he was. A week later there was his article that took up half the first page in the entertainment section in the daily newspaper entitled "Ray St. Germain's Problems with the CBC." It was filled with quotations I never said. For instance, "The CBC does not believe in the star system", "I don't even have my own dressing room", plus many other damning statements I never said. I couldn't believe what I was reading. I called him up and demanded a retraction. He said he stood by his article. It was only him and me during the interview.

I called the producer, Ray McConnell and expressed my concern. He told me this happens now and then during interviews and the CBC would understand. I was relieved but still worried. This T.V. critic could ruin my CBC show and my career if the Director of Programming thought there might be some truth to the article. It turned out I was right to worry about it.

On the ninth show I was to hear if the series would continue for the year or end at the end of the thirteenth episode. I was nervous during rehearsal of the 9th show but still didn't hear anything. Five minutes to show time, I was ready and waiting in the dressing room for the producer to call me to the stage. I was looking out the window from the second floor at the audience and cast all ready for show time when a knock came on the door. It was the Head of Programming! My heart raced a mile a minute in anticipation of what he was going to say. The producer called me over the intercom at the same time and said to make my way to the stage.

The Head of Programming said, "This won't take long." He told me the series was cancelled and I had until the thirteenth episode. My world came crashing down as I stood there in stunned silence. I finally asked, "Why?" He said the show had poor ratings. I suspected that, because I had asked earlier if the time slot could be moved because we were on at 8:30 pm Thursday nights against the *Dean Martin Hour* on CTV that started at 8pm. He offered no other excuse, but he did ask before he left the dressing room, "What did you mean when you said in the newspaper article, THEY at the CBC don't believe in the star system?" I didn't say that. I even had my own dressing room that originally belonged to Juliette! It didn't matter, I was through.

I headed down the stairs to the studio and began the show. It was hard to concentrate. Telling me five minutes before I had to perform? One of the Sinatra ballads I had to sing on that show was called "Cycles." It contained the words, "My gal just up and left last week, Friday I got fired." Also "Things can't get any worse than now" and "so I'll keep on trying to sing but please, just don't ask me now." I fought back tears, anger and rage. I sang sitting on a stool in the middle of the audience and really wanted to hit the smirky-looking fellow on my right.

That same year he also cancelled *The Don Messer Show* even though it was in the top ten watched shows in Canada at the time. The public was in an uproar over Don's Show. Funny, they never reacted that way to my cancellation. I didn't really expect them to.

Gene Telpner's *Winnipeg Tribune* said it best. "Pitting Ray St. Germain's show against Dean Martin was like Tiny Tim fighting Mohammed Ali."

My first concern was my family. How was I going to support them now?

Okay, time for a new plan. I could work the club circuit in and around T.O. and also write a new T.V. show and submit it to CBC. But the Head of Programming was still there. First I had to contact the Toronto Musicians' Union and get permission to work the clubs in T.O. After all, I was a member of the Winnipeg Local and the Musicians' Union was North American wide. Elvis was a member and every touring act that was professional had to be. Every professional that played an instrument had to be otherwise you couldn't perform on television or play with musicians that didn't belong.

However, each Local protected their players. You couldn't move from one location and immediately start making a living in another Local without a grace period. Toronto's was, I believe, three months at the time. Much to my surprise, they told me even though I had been in T.O. for fourteen weeks, I was on a traveling permit and would have to apply for the three months grace period. They knew my situation but wouldn't bend.

I told them I was just a singer that played guitar and would be no threat, believe me, to any guitar player in T.O. Maybe they thought because I was Lenny Breau's brother-in-law and had spent all that time on the road with him, I was a threat to Ed Bickert, one of the best in Canada at the time.

Tommy Hunter and Steve Hyde came to my rescue. We met at Tommy's home and he said he would help me write a new show. He said he would produce it if his contract wasn't renewed with the CBC. Juliette, Alex Trebeck and Bruce Marsh (the voice of Kraft) also were disturbed by what happened and had me on their

CBC radio show *Live at the Colonnade* to talk about my situation. Tommy's show was renewed and he told me to take the show we had written and submit it under my name.

In the meantime, the CBC gave me a one-hour special called *Two for the Road* with co-host Pat Harvey that would take us across Canada featuring local professional talent. So, all was not lost. The Head of Programming was human after all. Although, still to this day, I wish he had told me about the cancellation of *Time for Livin* a little differently.

The show I submitted to CBC was called *My Kind of Country* and featured Nashville stars taped in front of a live audience. Featuring Nashville stars hadn't been done on any show, to my knowledge, on the CBC at the time. Much to my delight, the CBC bought it! There was one catch; it was to be done in Winnipeg.

What? I moved my family to T.O. and sold our house! Were they trying to get me out of Toronto? I had no choice. Take it or leave it.

I drove back to Winnipeg alone to do the trial show. It was in January or February and my car froze up just outside of Kenora, Ontario, about 130 miles from Winnipeg. I got towed to Kenora and stayed in a hotel that asked me to sing in the lounge that night for my room. Why not? I also asked them to throw in supper and breakfast while my car thawed out in the garage.

We did the pilot in the CJAY Studios because their studio was bigger than the CBC Winnipeg studio. Ted Komar was the bandleader and Larry Brown produced the show. It was a success and it ran for twenty six weeks on the National Network with guest stars from Nashville such as Lefty Frizzell, Carl Smith, Jimmy C. Newman, Dave Dudley, Bobby Bare, Tom T. Hall, Connie Smith, Wilma Lee and Stoney Cooper and many more. The regulars on the show were Melody Renville, Dennis Olson and Al Weldon. By the second show Ron Halldorson, steel guitar player, had become the bandleader. The band

members were Dave Shaw (bass); Reg Kelln
(drums); Dave Jandrich (piano); Wally Diduck
(fiddle); Bernie Bray (harmonica); and a rhythm
guitar player by the name of Brian Whyte.

*1969 - Village Inn, Winnipeg before
leaving for Toronto*

Chapter 12
The Sting -1975

That's right, in 1975, there was a con artist who used us to line his pockets. It started in Regina where I was playing with the band at the Regina Inn at the Tiki Room. A big tall overweight man in his 60's who walked with a cane asked me if I would be interested in doing a show to raise money for a boys' home. He said that the Mercy Brothers, Al Cherny and the Allan Sisters from the *Tommy Hunter Show* already agreed to do the show. I accepted and signed the contract. By the way, he was not from Regina, but somewhere in the United States, we found out later. We did the first show in Moose Jaw at the arena and it was sold out. After the show he asked my drummer, Reg Kelln, to help him with the suitcase filled with money and load it in the trunk of his car.

The next night we played Regina and it was sold out too. He then had help again loading the suitcase of money into his car. The next morning we woke up in the Regina Inn thinking we were late for our next gig in Swift Current and phoned his office that he had set up three months earlier, but the phone was disconnected... Then we got the phone call from one of the two people he had hired from Regina and made signing officers for his company. They told me he had fled the night before to the United States with all the cash, and leaving them with all the bills, including our pay.

I had insisted we were paid half the money before we flew to Regina, so all was not lost. The detectives told us our return tickets were invalid because everything else was bogus.

We took a chance and went to the airport and the tickets were okay. We sat in the washroom and drank a bottle of Scotch between us and talked about this sting we were caught in. During this time a fellow walked into the washroom and asked if I was Ray St. Germain. He said there was a lady standing outside who wanted to talk to me. I went to meet her, not realizing I was about to meet the love of my life.

She was Glory Doerksen, one of the Miss Manitoba finalists. I had hosted the pageant for ten years at the Red River Exhibition, starting about 1965, and I was attracted to her from the first time I introduced her on stage. It was a passing fancy then because I was still married. But this time, I was going through a separation after fifteen years of marriage. By the way, my first wife, Barbara, was right to want to end it because I was still hurting after being fired from my 'Big Break' on CBC and was impossible to live with. I couldn't even stand myself. I had too much self-pity and booze.

Glory was working in Regina as the Manager of the Ponderosa Steakhouse, and we agreed to see each other as often as we could. I thought of her as my special angel sent from God to save me. But she lived in Regina and I was on the road. We had late night phone calls from wherever I was playing until I couldn't stand not being with her anymore. She finally moved back to Winnipeg to stay with her parents and we could see each other when I was back off the road.

After my divorce, I proposed to Glory while standing on the steps of the old Winnipeg Arena. At the time I was hosting the Miss Manitoba Pageant. She said, "Yes," but I would have to ask her parents, a strong Mennonite family.

Ray and Glory's wedding picture,
September 25th, 1976

Yikes! Here I was, a divorced father of three children, an entertainer, no money, lots of bills, fourteen years older than her and, by the way, what is a Metis?

Much to my surprise, her father, Jake, told me Glory loved me and that was good enough for him and gave me permission to marry his daughter, as long as it was in the Mennonite Church. Glory's mom, Rosabel, and brother Brad went along with it because of Jake, but they were going to keep their eyes on me.

We were married September 25th, 1976.

Chapter 13
Brian Whyte my half-brother

People used to ask me if Brian Whyte was my brother, because we looked alike. Brian and I had become good friends while working together on the show *My Kind of Country*, Brian on rhythm guitar and me hosting.

1970 – CBC, My Kind of Country Band,
½ Brother Brian Whyte 2nd from right,

He had confided in me how he had been raised to believe his grandparents were his mom and dad and his birth mother was his sister. He started searching for his father as soon as he found out the truth.

After what seemed like forever he managed to get the files opened up for him and he discovered his dad's name was Simon Adrien St. Germain from St. Vital. This would have been 1977, when I was 37 and he was 41.

I was playing at the Ramada Inn on Pembina Highway in Winnipeg when he and his wife came in and waited until the break to tell me. I was stunned. We embraced and cried. Here was a good friend who had told me many times about wanting to find his father when we were on the road playing shows. I always hoped his father was still alive and wished he could connect with him.

Brian's mother had been dad's girlfriend and when she got pregnant, her parents sent her away to have the baby. (This was four years before dad met my mom.) When she returned with baby Brian he was raised to believe his grandparents were his mom and dad and his birth mother was his sister.

I kept staring at him all through the gig and could see my father's and other brother Jesse's features. We went back to the house after, and I introduced my new-found brother to my new wife, Glory.

The next day I went to my parents' house to break the news. But how? I took my mom shopping and said to her in the car "Last night there was a woman in the lounge who said she knew dad before you did. I think her name was Leslie." (Brian's mom). My mom said, "You found Brian." I nearly drove off the road. I asked her to explain and she did. Mom knew that dad had fathered a child four years before they were married and because of that they almost didn't get married. Her dad, my Grandpa Ducharme, didn't approve and it seemed neither did Leslie. Mom and Dad thought she had moved away with Brian and that they would never be in contact with him anymore. So they never told my siblings and me.

Chapter 14
The Lounge

One night, the band and I were playing in Winnipeg at the Airliner lounge. It was a quiet Tuesday, with just a few salesmen were sitting at the bar, undressing the waitresses with their eyes, and in front near the bandstand and dance floor, four men were trying to have a conversation over the volume of the band. The band didn't play loud but they were quite close to the band. Suddenly, in through the door came a half-drunk woman, or was she half sober? She plunked herself down at the table of four men and stated quite loudly that she would like a drink and a dance or two. Or was it a dance and a drink or two? She then looked at me and commanded the band to play something good. Usually when someone in her condition requests something GOOD, they mean the simplest three chord song that has a lot of shouting in it. She must have danced at least five songs in a row and after each one she would come up to the bandstand and yell at me to play more.

We finally took a break and I walked by the table. Just as I was walking by she yelled at me, "Hey, you're Ray St. Germain!" I stopped and said "Yes I am, and how are you this evening?" as I reached out to shake her extended hand. And then she said it!!! "WHERE ARE YOU PLAYING THESE DAYS?"

Playing a lounge is one of the good gigs because it's in between a rowdy pub and an upscale nightclub. The lounge patrons are usually a loyal following and don't seem to mind hearing the same songs every night. In a lounge, you can play all kinds of music-pop, country, rock, jazz, Latin and the patrons will dance to it. In other words, you HAVE to be able to play it all. Of course, you play for all kinds of people from different walks of life.

Back to the Airliner lounge. It was a bitterly cold weekend in January, -30 Celsius (-24 Fahrenheit) as cold as only we in Winnipeg, Manitoba, Canada know it can be and getting colder. I left for work that night at 8:30 PM and it was going down to -40 Celsius, which at that point, becomes -40 Fahrenheit in any language.

Much to my surprise, the lounge was packed and noisy, waiting for us to start. The lounge held 150 people sitting down, 450 if you piled them on one another lying down. I'm sure that scenario ran through our bass player's mind. He just sometimes thought that way. We played the first set and on the break, I headed out to start my car to warm it up so it wouldn't freeze. On my way out, a man and a woman stopped me at their table and asked if I could help them out. He told me he was from The Pas and had a band called the *Lonely Hearts*. He asked if I could recommend a bass player to play up in The Pas. (The Pas is about three hundred miles or five hundred kilometers NORTH of Winnipeg). I thought of my own bass player 'cause he was in a snarly mood that night, but then said, "I can't think of one right now, but leave me your card and if anyone pops up I'll give it to them." Then I asked what happened to the previous bass player and he replied, "He more or less passed away" MORE OR LESS PASSED AWAY????

Another time the band and I were sitting near the exit on a break when a guy who had too much to drink staggered toward the door. He suddenly stopped, straightened himself up, turned to us and asked, "Pardon me sir, but is this the out entrance?" THE OUT ENTRANCE?

My old friend Brian Sklar, who is one of the best fiddle players in the country and a pretty good singer/songwriter, tells me of the time he and his band were playing in northern Saskatchewan at a hotel pub. It was a Saturday afternoon jam session where anyone in the pub can get up and sing with the band. On a break, a patron came up and said there was a pretty good singer in the audience and he should be called up to sing.

and then left the stage still glaring at Brian. On the break Brian went over to the fellow's table and asked what the matter was. "Why are you glaring at me?" The fellow got up, stared right into Brian's face, nose to nose, and said very slowly, "The group is called *SEA BREEZE*!!!"

"SOS Lounge" Birchwood and Holiday Inn
Paul Pododworny (drums), Denis Hammerstedt (guitar) and Ray

He was pointed out and Brian strolled over to talk to him. After the man figured out what he was going to sing, Brian asked how he should be introduced on stage. The fellow replied, "So and so from the group called *THREE BREEDS*". At least, that's what Brian heard, or thought he heard. Brian introduced so and so from the group called the *THREE BREEDS*. The fellow came on stage glaring at Brian, sang his song

Chapter 15
Jimmy King

Another good friend of mine, the late Jimmy King, one of the best-known bandleaders in our area, was the most colourful, interesting man you could ever meet in a lifetime. Jimmy never backed away from anyone or anything. He was a big man in size and personality. He stood about 6 feet 3 inches and weighed about 245 pounds. When he entered a room full of people they would automatically gravitate to him. If he had a few of the bubbly, as he was known to do on more than one occasion, he would shout "LET THE JOY BEGIN," and it usually did.

Jimmy King

Because Jimmy was so popular, you can imagine the stories. But this one is true. One night Jimmy was coming home from a gig. It was March, and Winnipeg in March can be a little dicey when it comes to the weather. There were still lots of snow banks on the side of the streets and Portage Avenue, one of the main thoroughfares, was a skating rink with ruts in the ice worn by the traffic.

Jimmy had stopped off at Harry Smith's Club Morocco on Portage Avenue to have a few last tastes (drinks) with his buddies and headed home at closing time. The ruts in the icy road were making his car weave and he noticed in the rear-view mirror a police car following. The more he tried to drive straight down the road, the more the ice tossed his car around. He finally came to his street and turned onto it. At the same time he gave it a little too much gas and went into a spin right into the snow bank. The police car was right behind him. On went the red lights. As Jimmy sat in his car, a young policeman came up to the window and asked, "Have you been drinking sir?" Jimmy replied, "Of course, son, what do you think I am? A DAMN STUNT DRIVER?"

One time at the Winnipeg Stadium during exhibition week, Jimmy was booked to back up the circus acts. A late arriving act needed to rehearse. The area where the acts performed was closed until performance time, but it was really an open area so people could still hear the band rehearsing. Jimmy wasn't too happy about having to rehearse this late act just before show time. What he didn't know was that the P.A. system was on for everyone to hear outside the performance area. The microphone stuck inside the top of the piano that Jimmy played was left open and picked up not only the piano, but Jimmy's remarks to the band and his mutterings to himself. The act was dancing dogs!! The music cues were whatever the dogs were wearing (dress, clown hat, etc). In other words, whenever the dog came on stage you had to play a certain piece of music according to what it wore.

All around the exhibition you could hear Jimmy cuing the band, turning pages, counting in tempos and cursing the dogs. "1-2-3-4 Now what the hell is this? 1-2-3- Is that a damned Clown's hat or a Shriner's thing? 1-2-1-2 What an ugly mutt. Man I hate dog acts!"

Jimmy was one of a kind, as they say about anyone who leaves a lasting impression on his fellow man or a disgruntled dog trainer.

Jimmy ("the King") and I would often attend the games of the Winnipeg Blue Bombers, our Canadian Football Team, where Jimmy was often mistaken for an ex-football player because of his size. Part of our outings would include Jimmy and me playing practical jokes on each other, if given the chance.

A week after cancer claimed Jimmy, I was asked to sing the Canadian National Anthem at a football game between Winnipeg and the Calgary Stampeders. I was a little apprehensive because I was born in 1940 and knew only the original words. (Some rocket scientist decided the words should be changed slightly in 1967, Canada's Centennial year.) You can understand the confusion and humming that went on whenever the anthem was required to be sung. The football club told me not to worry because the words came up on a billboard a line at a time. Everyone, including me, would be able to follow along easily except I would be standing at centre field with a microphone for all to hear. I don't know

why but I couldn't get Jimmy out of my thoughts that day.

The words started to roll by on the billboard and I raised my voice to sing loud and clear. Then it happened!! When the new words "From far and wide, O'Canada" were supposed to appear, and by this time I was counting completely on reading the words, the billboard went blank!!! There I was standing in the middle of 25,000 people feeling stark naked. I thought of Robert Goulet and his mangling of the American anthem. Then I thought I saw Jimmy in the stands laughing hysterically. Of course! He had pulled one last practical joke.

After the crowd stopped humming and laughing they gave me an ovation and a place in Winnipeg football history. It was the first time the billboard ever stopped during the singing of our national anthem.

They asked me back to redeem myself the next game. This time I took my ten year old son, D.J., out to the middle of the field and asked him to sing loud and clear so dad could hear every word. Even though I had rehearsed it until I knew it backwards, I wasn't about to take any chances. Even today when I'm asked to sing the anthem, I make sure I have the words hidden someplace where I can see them.

Chapter 16
Ray St. Germain Country/Big Sky Country

A new television station opened up in Winnipeg called CKND, September 1st, 1975. Izzy Asper and Associates owned it. The other stations operating in the 'Peg' at the time were CBC, French and English, and CKY. My buddy, Jimmy King and I approached the station with an idea for a Country and Western Talent Show in 1976-77. I would host and Jimmy would supply the band. They agreed and we produced thirteen shows that were shown locally. We were then asked to each produce and host our own series. Izzy Asper believed in Manitoba talent and thought there should be an outlet for gifted musicians and singers. Izzy himself was quite a jazz piano player.

In 1978, we did four shows on location at Dorothy and Les Loewen's place on south Waverley just outside of Winnipeg. Bill McAughy was brought in to direct the show. The show featured my daughters, Chrystal and Cathy, plus Wendy Halldorson, the daughter of bandleader Ron Halldorson, and his five-piece band, which included my long time friends, guitarist Denis Hammerstedt and drummer, Paul Pododworny. Bill Merritt was on bass and Jim McEachren on keyboard. I wrote the scripts, was the singing host and produced the shows. The shows had to work. They had to be sold to other TV stations throughout Canada if we were to even think about doing another series.

Much to my delight and CKND, the shows sold and even won the Gold Medal for Outstanding New Variety Program at the Can/Pro Awards held in Toronto for private TV productions. In 1979, we were asked to produce thirteen shows that would be played twice that year. And so it went on until 1990. Wow! Thirteen years counting 1978. Sold

Ray Jr., in the recording studio for his guest appearance on 'Ray St. Germain Country'

across Canada every year to private stations and networks. The show changed

1980 – Ottawa, Chateau Laurier (Left to Right) Denis Hammerstedt, Ted Mayor and Ray St. Germain

over the years with different co-hosts, Denis Hammerstedt becoming bandleader and my daughters leaving the show in 1983 but coming as guests from time to time.

It was hard to plan or book guests a year ahead because I wouldn't know if the series was sold for the upcoming season until February or March of that year. The shows had to be planned and audio recorded before we could videotape the series in June. I'm so grateful that CKND stuck with me all those years. Stan Thomas, Head of Programming, actor, producer and writer, was a tremendous help with his encouragement and guidance. He still is considered one of my best friends. The show was called *Ray St. Germain Country* and it stayed that way until CKND opened up two new stations in Regina and Saskatoon, Saskatchewan in 1986. I was asked to scout for Saskatchewan

1980 – Ray St. Germain

talent for the continuation of *Ray St. Germain Country,* only now to be called *Big Sky Country* because the series would be hosting and producing ten shows from Winnipeg, five shows from Regina and five shows from Saskatoon each year until the series ended in 1990. I still

can't believe the run I had. Thank you CKND (now Global) Izzy Asper, Stan Thomas, Peter Liba, Don Brinton, Al Bleichert, Heather (Reba) McIntyre and all the crew.

The shows were video taped mostly outdoors at locations we would find by driving around scouting outdoor sites that would look good on camera and fit the songs we were singing. I loved that part of the series. As soon as the snow melted, I would be in my car searching for locations. That was the beauty of the series. If you didn't like the songs or the singers, the scenery saved us. Soon everybody in the crew started suggesting locations they had found. Manitoba and Saskatchewan are blessed with some of the most beautiful outdoor museums on the planet.

We featured guests from all across Canada and even Nashville: Bobby Bare, Dave Dudley, Penny DeHaven, Stonewall Jackson, Jeannie C. Riley, Freddy Weller, Leroy Van Dyke, Jan Howard, Carol Baker, Terry Carrisse, Dick Damron, Family Brown, Gordie Tapp, Al Cherny, Michelle Wright, Tommy Cash,

Van for taping TV shows in Saskatchewan

(Johnny Cash's brother) and many more. We also featured lots of local singers every show.

In 1983, we did a series called *The Hits of Yesterday* and performed the hits from the years 1949 to 1961. My co-host was the multi-talented Ilena Zaramba and the series was shot at Skinner's Drive-Inn in Lockport, Manitoba. The Manitoba Antique Auto Club would send us an automobile from the year that we were featuring and we would feature the vehicle also.

The old part of Skinner's was still standing and we decorated it with old Coca-Cola signs and even an old hand-pump gas stand. We also wore clothes from the "50's". It was one of the most enjoyable series I ever did.

*Ray's daughters, Chrystal and Cathy
on 'Ray St. Germain Country'*

*1990 - Ray St. Germain and
The Big Sky Band
(Left to Right) Paul Kelly, Daryl Gutheil (of Streetheart),
Ray Jr., Ray, Angie Carriere, Paul Pododworny*

Cathy, Ray and Chrystal 'Ray St. Germain Country' at Ray's Farm in Oakbank, Manitoba

On location 'Ray St. Germain Country'
Red River Ralph, Ray and Cousin Clem (Gordie Tapp)

The Farm
Chapter 17

In 1980, Glory and I purchased our Ponderosa, all five acres, three miles west of Oakbank, Manitoba on Pine Ridge Road. It had just what we needed for our television series, and we lived there for five years. Beside the house, there was the Green Barn (that needed to be painted, red with white trimming), plus a one-room log cabin and a two-room guesthouse, all needed to be refurbished. So our "green acres" saga began... A Metis guy from the city, pretending to know his roots, and a Mennonite girl from Winkler, raised in the city. Yep, we were definitely "Green Acres".

DJ riding his pony Caramel

T

Neighbours Wally and Wanda Comrie helping with horses for TV show

Thank goodness for Wally and Wanda Comrie, our new neighbors, and their daughters, Sara and Morgan, (especially Wanda) who taught us how to survive thirty miles out of the city.

Her mom and dad, Walter and Anne Conklin lived next door, and just laughed and scratched their heads, watching us city folk pretending to be country folk.

We taped the *Ray St. Germain Country*

"The Red Barn"
Party with Denis, Ray (on drums) and Paul performing for friends before taping 'Ray St. Germain Country'

television series there for one year, as well as a few other shows. We even purchased a few horses "Penny and Keyhole" from Wanda and Wally, and "Carmel" from Warren and Gail Loos. Warren and I wrote a song together called the "Old Leather Halter." Warren wrote the words and I wrote the music. Tom and Brenda Tallman tapped their toes. Wow, we were really living the country life! The Metis and the Mennonite! We called our kids M & M's. Our daughter Sherry-Rose was born in 1981 while we lived there. So now we were set.

Five acres of land, two young children, three horses, a dog and a cowboy hat.

We had lots of fun, especially shooting the opening of the television show. My daughter Cathy was riding a pony we borrowed from Wanda (who lived across the rode). While taping the opening of the show the director suggested we gallop out of the driveway. (Never let a horse run in the direction of home). The director shouted "action" and we all galloped down the driveway towards the road, except for the horse Cathy was riding, which ran all the way home, right into the barn with Cathy still hanging onto the horn of the

Ray Jr. on his horse Cinamin

saddle, and just ducking as her horse entered the barn. Cathy hopped off and stormed out of the barn yelling, "Dad, I hope they got that cause I'm not doing that again!" Ahh yes, the life of a cowboy.

Our neighbor Walter loved to watch the goings onof the farm, but he liked things done right and kept in order. He always asked me to clean up the old stove, that was leaning against the outside of the barn, facing his machine shed.

He kept an old fridge in there to keep his beer cold, and every now and then we'd chat as he'd head out to his machine shed to have a "cold one"

Ray riding 'Keyhole'

from the fridge and remind me of the "eyesore" stove that really should be moved. So, one day I did move it. Since he always commented on it I thought I'd park it right in front of his beer fridge inside the machine shed. One day while he was out working in the field I did just that, and then waited for him to come home, anticipating his reaction.

A few days passed and no word from Walter. I was a little concerned; perhaps I had annoyed him with my little practical joke. So I went over to see how he was doing. "Hey Walter," I said, "How'd you enjoy the gift I left you in front of your beer fridge?" "Oh, great," he said. "Thanks, I sold that old stove for $50.00 and filled up my beer fridge". We both had a good laugh, and many more jokes were played on each other while we lived there.

Chapter 18
Overseas Tour – 1983

My wife Glory sent in a proposal to the Department of National Defence for the Ray St. Germain Show to entertain troops in Germany, Israel and Cyprus. We got the show and were to present a Christmas show in 1983. The shows usually came from Toronto, Montreal or Edmonton. It was a first for Winnipeg.

We had to have Vegas-style dancers and variety acts. The show had to be 40% French language. We included my daughter, Cathy, and her band, *The Rage*, who would back up most of the acts.

Cathy St. Germain and The Rage, performing for the UN troops.

Our M.C. was Vincent Derrault and we had a mime act, magician Brian Glow and my old friend Denis Hammerstedt and his wife, Edie, plus technical crew and sound, (Tom Kowalski) and lights (Christie Wigston). Altogether we had a cast and crew of about twenty-four people.

We flew to Lahr, Germany and almost lost Brian Glow there when we stopped at a bank to exchange our money before heading to the base. Everyone got

Christie Wigston (lighting technician) loading the UN trucks with equipment for the show. Or was that just her luggage?

back on the bus at the bank except for Brian, who was in the manger's office talking about exchange. Glory and I were picked up in a car and driven to the base ahead of the rest.

Germany, (Left to Right) Major Roberge, Tom Kowalski and Brian Glow (who we left at the bank! Sorry Brian.)

The bus arrived at the base and we were taken to a reception. We were all excited about being there and forgot to take a head count. About an hour later, Brian walked in, fuming. He told us he had one heck of a time getting to the base. He had to take a cab and when he got to the check point at the base they wouldn't let him pass because they didn't have his name. I think he finally did a few magic tricks and he was let in. From then on, a head count was taken everywhere we went.

Brian Glow, the magician
(Yep, the one that got left behind)

The Armed Forces, families and friends attended the show. What an ovation we received! We ended the show with "I'll Be Home For Christmas" and there wasn't a dry eye in the house, including us.

We had a few days off and they took us on sightseeing trips to Switzerland and France.

Our next show was in Baden. It was a thrill arriving and seeing a big billboard "Welcome the Ray St. Germain Show to Baden" on the highway.

We then flew to Israel. We landed in Tel Aviv and started to unload the Hercules aircraft when, much to my horror, my guitar came off cracked down the middle starting at the bridge. It had been laid flat when loaded and luggage piled on top of it. The case looked like a spoon. I wanted to yell and scream because I had taken a chance by not bringing a back-up guitar as all traveling musicians should. Because of the armed Israeli soldiers watching us, I yelled softly. That Ovation guitar is now on display at the Canadian Country Music Hall of Fame in

Calgary. I sang the shows just holding the guitar while the band backed me up.

(Left) Robin Dow, dancer, flying on the
Hercules to Baden, Baden

We stayed in a five-star hotel in Tiberius on the Sea-of- Galilee. We all had beautiful rooms except there wasn't a television. I called down to the desk and they said I could rent one. They had two channels, Tel Aviv and one from Jordan with some English programs. We rented one and they brought it to our room and set it up. When they turned it on, the first picture we saw was Sherrise Laurence singing on the show she co-hosted called *Circus*. What a surprise! Especially since I had just signed her before we left to be my co-host on the seventh season of *Ray St. Germain Country* on Global T.V. *Circus* ran a number of years on the CTV network and was now over but packaged and sold all over the world.

Our first show was in the Golan Heights near the border of Syria on Christmas Day, and it was also Glory's birthday. We sang a lot of Christmas songs and cried again. Our son D.J. was three years old and our daughter, Sherry was just one year old. They were at home staying with Glory's parents. It was very difficult to do the show as we kept thinking of them every second we were there.

We all bought puzzle rings from Damascus and Glory and I still wear ours today as a reminder of that bittersweet Christmas.

We had a few days off after that and they took us to Bethlehem where we saw the Holy Shrine where Jesus was born. We also went to Jerusalem and walked the Way of the Cross. The street where Jesus carried his cross to his crucifixion and the seven stops along the way where he fell. We also went to the Great Western Wall (the Wailing Wall).

On the way back we stopped at the Dead Sea and the River Jordan at the place where Jesus was baptized by John. It was something we'll always remember and brought us all closer together.

We left Israel for Cyprus next. This beautiful island in the Mediterranean Sea was divided by war. The Greeks were on one side and the Turks on the other. They were kept from resuming the war by a fragile truce enforced by the United Nations of which Canada played such an important part. The Canadian Peacekeepers were greatly respected all over the World, and certainly here.

We stayed in Nicosia and were taken on a tour of the Green Line, the line dividing the warring factions and patrolled by the United Nations. The Canadians were the best at this. The line became a narrow street when it entered Nicosia. On each side of the street, on top of the buildings, were the manned, armed bunkers, the Greeks on one side of the street and the Turks on the other. The buildings looked like they were from a war movie, full of bullet holes and signs hanging half off.

We were all a little nervous and curious as we rode in the back of three clearly marked United Nations half-ton trucks. All of a sudden, two Turkish soldiers armed with rifles jumped out in front of our convoy and ordered us to stop. The officer with us ordered the drivers to keep going. WHAT?! They have guns! They stepped aside and let us continue on our way. The officer explained they could take our passports if we complied with their command. He would report this when we got back to headquarters.

Bunkers in Israel

I still expressed my concerns to the Commanding Officer and he assured me the officer did the right thing. Still, I thank God the Turkish soldiers did not have a hang-over or felt the need to start shooting.

That wasn't the only adventure we had in Cyprus. Glory and I ate fried goat cheese in the restaurant before we were to attend a reception for us all at the Canadian Consulate. Funny how something you never tried before tastes so-o-o- good and then makes you sicker than a dog in a matter of an hour. We missed the reception and asked my daughter, Cathy, to leave us the key to her room as we would need two bathrooms. Cathy later said the party was wonderful and she represented us well. Of course she did! She's my daughter.

The next adventure involved a car. A young soldier said I could borrow his car if I had an International Driver's License. I had got one before we left just in case this opportunity came along. It was the weekend and we were told the most beautiful beaches in the world were located on the other side of the island. So, Glory and I plus two others from the cast decided to go there. First, I had to practice driving a right-hand drive vehicle on the left side of the road. That's right-think the opposite of how you've been driving all your life. After hitting the curb a few times and getting caught in a traffic circle, I figured we were ready to venture to the other side of the island through the mountains. We were warned not to wander off the beaten path and get lost on the Turkish side because that would be bad for us.

Along the way we needed fuel and it was also starting to rain. We stopped at a restaurant and asked where the nearest place we could get fuel would be. They pointed to a little road off the BEATEN path and away we went. After many miles down this little road we came to a village. I stopped at what I thought was a gas station and asked if I could get fuel. They did not speak English. Through sign language of sorts the woman brought a gallon jug of gas pumped from a barrel. She made many trips and we paid too much as I could not understand the price. I just took out my money and she took $60.00 American and smiled. When we pulled out of there we decided maybe we should go back to Nicosia, but somewhere I made a wrong turn…

That's right, we were lost in the mountains driving on a dirt road that clung to the side of the mountain. We could see villages way down below and would eventually make our way to them in the pouring rain only to find out nobody understood us. All we could say was "Nicosia? Nicosia?" They would nod and point in the direction of another road and up the mountain we would go again. It was getting dark and when w e got into another

Ray driving a car in Cyprus

village I decided to just follow a road that looked well traveled on. We all kept thinking we were on the Turkish side and would never be heard from again. Then we came to a crossroad and a sign that pointed left and said Nicosia. It was dark and I was sure all the headlights coming towards us were on the wrong side of the road which they weren't. It was nerve-wracking but we made it back and I never drove the car again.

We were away from the middle of December, 1984 to the middle of January, 1985 and I don't think any of us would trade that experience for any other trip. When we landed in Ottawa, we all kissed the ground and realized what a great country Canada is.

The adventure did not stop in Ottawa. No, it continued in Winnipeg. All of our sound equipment, lights, amplifiers, drums and anything like clothes trunks, etc.were to be transported by truck to Winnipeg. It would arrive a few days later. I got a call that our equipment had arrived but there was a problem… Glory and I were asked to go to a hangar and we would be told what the problem was when we got there. Every piece of equipment had been taken apart and was scattered all over the hangar floor with a lot of people going through every piece.

This is what happened. Denis Hammerstedt, guitar player, comedian (Red River Ralph), married to Edie (make-up artist) and good friend and I would do a skit on stage that involved a bottle of Coca Cola and a small clear package that contained icing sugar. He had a few in case he lost some. The skit would go something like this:

Remember that 7-Up commercial in the '80's that featured a black man in a white suit and hat that ended with "What goes with rum down in the islands? 7-Up", or something like that. Denis would do the commercial and hold up that little package of icing sugar and instead of saying 7-Up, he would say "coke". I would yell at him and he would then hold up a Coca-Cola bottle. It always got big laughs. You had to see it.

His trunk that contained all the comedy hats and stuff also contained the Coca-Cola bottles and little packets of icing sugar. It seems that during the transporting of Denis's trunk during that cold January, the Coca-Cola bottles exploded and were leaking all over the trunk. When they unloaded the equipment they opened the trunk only to find the leaking bottles and what looked like packets of Cocaine. That was it! Everything had to be taken apart and the packets analyzed. By the time we got there, they said everything was fine now and we explained the act. It all ended well.

Overseas Christmas Show,
The entire cast

Loading the bus for the Northern Tour

Ray riding a camel in Israel

Rehearsing on the bus

Chapter 19
Canadian Armed Forces Tour – 1987

In 1987, the Ray St. Germain Show was booked by the Canadian Armed Forces to entertain the troops throughout Northern Canada. We took a cast of about 25 entertainers, musicians and crewmembers and once again flew on a Hercules to Goose Bay, Labrador, Alert, then in the Northwest Territories, now Nunavut, Yellowknife, NWT and Massett, the Queen Charlotte Islands off the coast of British Columbia.

It was in November and we were issued Artic gear mainly because of the weather in Alert. It was situated on the northern tip of Ellsmere Island about two hundred miles from the North Pole. At that time of year it had twenty-four hours of darkness.

Now I understand the need for Military time. Showtime was 19:00 hours or 7:00 PM. It was quite an experience although I had been up there in the late '60's' with the CBC. But this time, it was "our" show co-produced by my wife, Glory.

We were told that, when walking outside, we should always wear our Arctic gear and hang onto ropes connecting the buildings because a white-out could suddenly happen without warning and we wouldn't be able to see anything. The buildings were built on stilts and the dreaded Artic Fox loved to stay under them. I say dreaded because we were told some had rabies and under no circumstances were we to go near them. If they bit you it could be fatal because it could be a long time before a plane could fly up to rescue you. I thought, "What about our Hercules?" They meant DON'T TOUCH!

We were there for three days, and one night I was partying it up with the cast and the Armed Forces people and decided to go back to our barracks. I got outside and walked down the steps to follow the rope and I slipped.

As I lay there, embarrassed because I didn't wear my Artic boots, I saw them coming for me. ARCTIC Foxes coming for dinner! I got up and screamed at them but they just kept coming! I ran as fast as I could to the building, hanging onto the rope and slipping and sliding all the way. The crew was standing on the steps, laughing hysterically.

When we left Alert, we were told to put our luggage outside the barracks and it would be picked up and loaded on the plane. We could only stand and watch and yell at the foxes while they peed on our luggage.

We arrived in Yellowknife and did the show and then headed off to Massett, Queen Charlotte Islands and our final show. We were taken on a tour of the Haida First Nations beautiful rainforest. We got to see the sacred Golden Pine tree standing as it had for over a hundred years. It stood shimmering a gold colour amongst a sea of green. (I understand a mad man cut it down a few years ago and he was never found.)

They also took us fishing for Steelhead in a fast moving stream. They gave us hip-waders that went all the way up to our chest. I went too far into the middle of the stream and the water was up to my waist. I guess you know by now that I'm not a fisherman. Our hosts were yelling at me to get back but I couldn't hear them because of the rushing water. One of them came out to get me and guide me back to shore. He said if I had snagged a Steelhead, a huge fish, it would drag me down, my hip-waders would fill up and I would pretty much drown. I thanked him and said I was finished for the day and he agreed. Do you believe in Guardian Angels? I sure do.

The night before we were to leave Masset for Winnipeg, we had a cast party in the hotel where the cast stayed. I stayed in a military house across a large body of water connected by a bridge.

At the end of the night I went to the front desk to call for a taxi. They told me the taxi service ended at midnight and it was now 12:05 AM. Just then, a man who was sitting in the lobby asked me if he could give me a ride. He then asked me if I was at the loud party. I said "Yes" and told him about the show. I got in his car and we started for the bridge. There was something telling me to get out and run as fast as I could.

As we drove onto the bridge he slowed down and asked if a girl by the name of, I forget now, was there. I said, "No, only the cast." He then proceeded to tell me his wife had left him and he thought she was partying at the hotel. He said he wanted to end his life. Oh great! I asked him if he believed in God and prayer. He said it never helped. I finally convinced him to pray together for help getting his wife back. He prayed for that and I prayed silently to get this car over the bridge.

When we reached the other side I told him it was the first house on the right. It wasn't, but I had to get out. He pulled into the driveway! I got out and thanked him and walked to the back of the house. I peeked around the corner to see if he was still there and he was. I thought, 'I'll wait all night if I have to.' He finally left and I got home safely. My Guardian Angel?

The adventure wasn't over. The next morning we were to fly home to Winnipeg, but when we watched on television we saw that Winnipeg was brought to a standstill by a huge snowstorm. No traffic was moving because of the blizzard. We boarded and were asked if we wanted to land in Edmonton and wait until the streets were cleared. They said they could land at the military base in Winnipeg but they couldn't get us home and we would be stuck in the terminal instead of a warm hotel room in Edmonton. The cast all agreed to go to Winnipeg. We'd been on tour for two weeks and wanted this to end.

When we landed we were told to hand back our Arctic gear. What? We need it now. When we left, we gave our winter clothes to our spouses who would meet us when we returned. The army said they could get down Portage Avenue, Main Street and a few other essential routes that had one lane clear. We all packed into troop carriers sitting in the back with only a canvas covering and no heat. They took us as close to our homes as they could.

I was dropped off at Portage and Westwood Drive. I had on a sports jacket, turtleneck and cowboy boots. Of course, I had pants on, but no winter underwear or gloves. I also had my guitar, suitcase, clothes bag and a four foot frozen salmon the Armed Forces people had given me because I didn't catch one. Home was five blocks away...the snow was up to my waist and even deeper where it drifted. I started to walk and crawl pushing my cargo ahead of me. Then out of the blue came two fellows on snowshoes who helped me home. Where did they come from at that precise time? I didn't get their names because I was so cold I could hardly ring the doorbell. My wife hugged me and said she had a warm bath waiting. The kids wanted to know what I brought them. I gave them the salmon.

I know this sounds strange, but Glory didn't see anyone with me at the door. Was I hallucinating? Or was it my Guardian Angels? I know they were Metis. Yes, I'm a firm believer.

Chapter 20
Ramada Inn

A new chapter in my life was about to begin. I still played road gigs for a while until I signed to play the Ramada Inn on Pembina Highway in Winnipeg for an extended stay. The owner, Bob Leslie, was a terrific man to work for. He allowed me to take time off for big shows that would come my way from time to time, as long as I had someone who could fill in for me. We worked the lounge six days a week and would pack in a regular crowd. I always managed to have great players with me such as Kas Siwik, Reg Kelln, Denis Hammerstedt, Ted Mayor, Paul Pododworny, Paul Kelly, Bill & Allen McDougall plus others. Sherisse Laurence or Hector Bremner would fill in for me when I needed time off. We became friends with the regular crowd and it was a wonderful time in my life.

One night, it was packed and there was a lineup to the front doors of the hotel when one of the waitresses came up to the bandstand and said Lorne Green was standing in line signing autographs, wanting to come in. Sure enough, there he was, with Bill McAughy, a film producer I had worked with. Bill introduced me and Lorne remembered that I had hosted a Winnipeg segment of a television special called *Canada for the Fun of it* of which he was the national host in Toronto. He had introduced my segment without ever meeting me.

He was in town working for Bill on a documentary and when Bill suggested going to the Ramada after the shoot to watch me perform, Lorne agreed. We got them in and they stayed until well after closing time.

What a great man "Pa Cartwright" was to talk with.

We played the "Ram" or "Wrinkles South" for about ten years off and on. ("Wrinkles West" was the Holiday Inn Airport West lounge where Al Andrusko played.) The average audience age was between thirty and fifty. I don't remember seeing any wrinkles in the audience but the "kids" were found mostly in the pubs.

Holiday Inn Airport West - 1998

Red River Ralph – Ramada Inn

Chapter 21
I Quit the Road

In 1990, the Big Sky Country nationally syndicated television series came to an end after thirteen years and some two hundred shows. I always wondered when it would. But by then, music videos had burst onto the scene and the other television stations were no longer buying shows like mine across Canada. CKND had given me a tremendous run and I was thankful but sad to see it come to an end. The Tommy Hunter Show also came to an end about the same time on CBC.

I ended up traveling on the road again doing fairs and rodeos across Western Canada with the *Big Sky Band*. We even did the Big Valley Jamboree in Craven, Saskatchewan and received a standing ovation from 20,000 people. What a thrill that was. My son, Ray Jr., said it was something he'll never forget. I told him maybe the crowd was happy we were finished so they could now see Lorrie Morgan who was next on the show.

We were booked to perform for the National Fair Association in Vancouver and also took a booking at the Sandman Inn while we were there. One night I started thinking about my young children back home and remembered how I missed my older children growing up while I was on the road. I even missed my oldest daughter's birthday every year because she was born July 10th, right in the middle of fair and exhibition season. I also was on the road when she was born. I missed most of my daughter Cathy's birthdays. She was born August 3rd, again traveling season. Ray Jr. was born in November so I caught most of his birthdays.

I called the band up to my room and told them I was going to quit the road. I was fifty years old and wanted to be at home with my wife and children. I wanted to see D.J. (nine years old) and Sherry (seven years old) grow up.

I needed to be at home with Glory. Besides, I was tired and fed up with all the traveling and staying in hotel rooms. I was also tired of performing. It wasn't a snap decision, I had been thinking about it for a while. On the flight home I felt relieved I had finally made my decision.

For the next few months I was able to attend my son's hockey games and my daughter's basketball games. I drove them to school and was about as happy as any father could be. I was on an extended holiday.

But I had to work somewhere. The money we saved was being dipped into more and more. I did a few small gigs but my heart was not into entertaining anymore.

I had attended a Vocal Coaching Clinic in Toronto back in 1959 and had practiced what they taught me through most of my career. In the meantime, Roy Petty, a great singer, was coaching singers in Winnipeg as he, too, had quit the road. Roy got sick and I called our mutual friend, Terry Morris, who is a booking agent, and asked if Roy was going to continue coaching. If not, I would be interested in buying his client list. And so, I started vocal coaching in my basement studio. I had thirty students a week including good friend Laureen "Sparky" Reeds, who now uses my vocal studio as her piano teaching studio. Her husband Dr. Paul Bullock a Professor at the University of Manitoba is also a singer with the award winning Harlequin Quartet.

That old feeling started to gnaw at me and I wanted to sing again. I took weekend jobs at the Holiday Inn Airport West lounge, filling in for Al Andrusco. I quit vocal coaching and tried to make a living entertaining in Winnipeg without having to go on the road. There just wasn't enough work like there used to be for acts like mine.

So, I got a real job. I sold cars for Eastern Sales and Westport Chrysler. I had some people come on the lot and ask me when I bought into the dealership. I lasted about a year. I missed singing way too much. I started to work more at the Holiday Inn lounge and really enjoyed singing with Denis Hammerstedt on guitar, Paul Pododworny on drums and Daryl Gutheil on keyboards.

In 1998 I joined the Manitoba Metis Federation to find out more about the organization and my people. I also got involved with the Indian and Metis Friendship Center and was inducted into the Aboriginal Wall of Honour. I was then asked by the Manitoba Metis Federation's newly elected President David Chartrand, and at the urging of then Lieutenant-Governor of Manitoba, Yvon Dumont, to start a radio show called *The Metis Hour*. We started it at CKJS in Winnipeg. We were there for a little while when NCI-FM moved here from Thompson, Manitoba. We then moved the show to NCI in 1999. We're still on the air, only now expanded to two hours every Saturday at 11:00 AM with David Chartrand, President of the Manitoba Metis Federation and my co-host, a very talented young lady by the name of Naomi Clarke. One of the highlights was having guests such as Premier Gary Doer come in and sing live, "I'm So Lonesome I Could Cry", or part of it at least. Actually, he sings pretty good...but he shouldn't try to make a living at it...
That's right, two days. On the third day she told me I was on my own. Sink or swim Television Star. We became life-long friends after that.

It wasn't long before NCI moved into a building at 1507 Inkster Blvd. The programming now came from Winnipeg except

NCI had its Winnipeg studios on St. James Street across from Polo Park and the CEO was Ron Nadeau. Half the day programming still came from Thompson. Ron asked me if I would like to host the drive show from 4:00 PM to 6:00 PM, Monday to Friday. Me? A radio disc jockey? The only experience I had in radio was one year way back in 1968 at the CBC when I co-hosted a show with Murray Parker called *Afternoon from Winnipeg* with the Bob McMullin Orchestra. The show was scripted and produced by Jack Bingham. All I had to do was sing and read the odd script. Murray carried most of the show.

I had a lot of friends in radio and I called them for help. And help they did. Mike McCourt and his wife Lorraine were close friends. Mike had started in radio in Saskatoon and he went on to be a television correspondent with ABC News after a stint with the CBC. He came to the rescue and coached me how to become a radio personality. Good friends, Bob Washington and Jim Coghill, also gave me a lot of tips.

You see, performing in front of an audience and talking to them is easy for me. I'd been doing it all my life. But to sit in front of a microphone staring at a window while talking is frightening. Is anybody listening? Where is the reaction to what I'm saying? Even on television you have the crew who would smile and give you the thumbs up. Mike suggested I put a picture of my wife in front of me. That worked for a while until I started arguing with the picture. I'm kidding. It actually worked.

When I started working at NCI, Dave McLeod was my supervisor. Naomi Clarke trained me on the board for two days.
for the Saturday Loonie Pot Bingo. It still came from Thompson under the direction of Eleanor Kee, the financial officer. Ron Nadeau, CEO, Dave McLeod, General Manager, myself Program Manager and host of the *Road Show* from 3:00 PM to 6:00 PM. (NCI can now be

heard on the World Wide Web – www.ncifm.com. Check out the website.)

I have had the privilege of working with people at NCI who bring a lot of experience in broadcasting such as: Bill Flamond, 40 years plus and an expert in country trivia; Gerry Barrett, also a successful standup comedian; Jasmine, Music Director; Cowboy Carl Thomas, The Iron Man of NCI; who puts in a lot of hours; Kimberley Dawn, a great singer; Newsman "The Voice" Robert Rahn; The always entertaining Cory "Coyote" Whitford, Rez Nation; Elijah Moose, Shylo Jones, Sid Minuk, The Automotive Hotline and so many others who have probably joined the NCI Network by now.

NCI-FM is the largest Aboriginal Radio Network in Canada and supports Aboriginal artists. NCI also has the biggest Aboriginal Amateur talent contest anywhere. It sells out the Centennial Concert Hall in Winnipeg every year.

I owe a huge debt of gratitude to the NCI Management and board. But most of all, I thank the Manitoba Metis Federation and President David Chartrand for starting me on my radio broadcasting career.

I would also like to thank Lisa Meeches for asking me to be the voice of the "Bear" on the award-winning children's program *Tipi Tales*. She also produced a documentary on my career for *The Sharing Circle* shown on APTN. By the way, not only is she extremely intelligent and beautiful, she is also a beacon of light for Aboriginal People. She is one of the most fascinating people I have ever met.

Yvon Dumot, Rick Kizuk and I produced a television series called *Rhythms of the Metis* for APTN showcasing Metis music and culture. The series is in English and French.

The Honorable Eric Robinson, Minister of Culture, Heritage and Tourism for the Manitoba Government, was also responsible for the *Aboriginal Express*, a show that Glory and I produced featuring Buffy Handel and her Indian Pearl Productions showcasing Aboriginal dances and songs. He suggested we take this show to southern parts of the province. It was a resounding success in 2004-05. I thank him for his support and belief that this would work. The show was always accepted at the fairs with standing ovations. There was only one incident that happened that was actually kind of funny.

The chartered bus was waiting in front of my house to load the equipment and the performers when the pow-wow drum group showed up in a small car. I walked up to the car and asked the four of them if the drum was already on the bus. They looked at each other and realized they had forgotten the huge pow-wow drum. I said, "What! That's your gig! That's what you do! You need the drum to perform! When you all crammed into the small little car, didn't you realize something was missing?" We all started laughing and two of them went back for the drum. They met us in time for the show…this time with the drum.

Epilogue

I'm still performing and in 2004 my CD called "My Many Moods" on Arbor Records was named Best Country Album in Milwaukee at the Indian Summer Music Awards. It contains a collection of songs I recorded over the years including my first recording with Lenny Breau on Chateau Records called "She's so Square".

I was also inducted into the "Manitoba Aboriginal Music Hall of Fame" in 2005 along with Errol "C-Weed" Ranville, Len Fairchuck, Ernest Monais, Lucille Starr and Robbie Brass. It is housed at NCI-FM in Winnipeg. You can also take a virtual tour online once again at www.ncifm.com.

There are so many people that had a profound impact on my life. I know that I've probably forgotten to mention some of them: Bob "Moose" Jackson, (now there's a book I'd like to read), Gordie Komosky, Reg Kelln, Marsh Phimister, Donnie Young, Ken Jefferson, Uncle Joe, Cousin Roland, Al Shorting, Jeff Bone, well, the list goes on and on.

The biggest and best accomplishments in my life, though, are my children, Chrystal, Cathy, Ray Jr., D.J. (David Joseph) and Sherry Rose. I have been blessed to have these wonderful children. They are all in the entertainment business with singing styles all their own. My daughter, Chrystal, has given me four beautiful grandchildren, Jeff, Jordon, Catie and Cody. They all sing too. My son-in-law, Rob Roy, is a very patient man.

The love of my life, Glory, is just what the good Lord ordered for me. How did he know? She is my "Special Angel" who saved me at the darkest moment in my life and stuck with me until I got it right. What a remarkable woman.

Thanks to my mom and dad for always believing in me and loving me no matter what. Also to my sisters, Val and Judy and their families plus my dearly departed brothers, Jesse, who left us way too soon, and Brian Whyte and their families.

Yeah, I wanted to be Elvis when I was younger but I wouldn't trade my life for his. Besides, he never got to stay at the Harwood Hotel in Moose Jaw.

Major Awards

Aboriginal Order of Canada – Ottawa

Aboriginal Wall of Honour - Winnipeg Friendship Centre

Order of the Sash - Saskatoon & Prince Albert

Manitoba Association of Country Arts (MACA)

    - Entertainer of the year

    - Song of the year

    - Male Vocalist

    - Recording Artist.

Golden Award – Recognition for lifetime achievement

Country Music Hall of Fame Display – Calgary

Best Country Album - "My Many Moods" Milwaukee Indian Summer Music Awards

Manitoba Aboriginal Music Hall of Fame

Native Council of Canada

Be it known to all that

Ray St. Germain

in recognition and appreciation of
outstanding and dedicated service to
Canada's Aboriginal Peoples, is hereby
recognized and affirmed as a

Member of the
Aboriginal Order of Canada

this 21st day of June 1985
at the 13th Annual Assembly of the
Native Council of Canada

Ottawa

Louis Bruyere
President

Harry W. Daniels
Vice President

Dwight A. Dorey
Vice President

Discography

1958 – She's A Square (Chateau – Single)

1958 – If You Don't Mean It (Chateau – Single)

1968 – Ray St. Germain L.P. (RCA Canadian Talent)

1969 - Time For Livin(L.P. Capital)

1978 - Ray St. Germain(L.P. Sunshine)

1979 - The Metis (Gigi Records – single)

Sweet Innocence (Gigi Records)

1980 - Show Me The Way (Rayne Records)
Memories, Memories (Rayne Records)

1983 - Ray St. Germain Live (L.P. – Rayne)

1985 – Thank God, I'm Metis (L.R. – Independent)

1990 – There's No Love Like Our Love (L.P. Broadland)

1996 – Ray St. Germain Greatest Hits – Vol. 1

2003 – My Many Moods (Arbor)

2005 – Ray St. Germain Family Christmas (Arbor)

Ray and Glory

Glory and Ray
Glory's 50th Birthday singing 'Jackson'

Ray and Glory's
Engagement
picture

Glory and Ray - 1980

Glory and Ray
Golan Heights, Israel - 1984

Ray and Glory on vacation

Ray and Glory at the airport (Always early)

Ray and Glory enjoying Winterpeg weather

Miss Manitoba Pagent float in parade. Glory center in white

Ray and Glory riding the bombardeer

Shall we dance? Glory and Ray, Margaret and Ted Motyka (instructors) and Laureen Reeds and Paul Bullock taking dancing lessons

Glory and Ray 2005

Family Pictures

Family Photo, Ray and Glory's 25th Anniversary
(Back Row) Cathy, Chrystal, Ray, Glory, Sherry
(Front Row) Ray Jr. and DJ

Ray, sisters Val and Judy, dad, mom and brother Jesse

Ray and family at Christmas - 1982

Ray and brother Jesse

Half-brother Brian Whyte and wife Darlene

Family Performance
(Left to Right)Ray, sons, DJ, Ray Jr., grandson Jeff,
daughters, Sherry and Cathy

*DJ, (Ray's son)(Right) performing with
Eagle and Hawk in Toronto for the
Aboriginal Music Awards - 2005*

*Carrying on the family tradition
(Left to right) DJ and granddaughter Catie - 2005*

Glory's brother Brad, wife Hilda, Glory's mom and cousin Adeline

Ray Jr. and Willie Nelson in Nashville

*Ray Jr. and Ray performing at Legends
in Nashville*

*Chrystal, Glory and Cathy going
Ski-doing*

Chrystal, Cathy, Sherry and granddaughter Catie at piano

Chyrstal and Cathy performing with Ray

'The Brothers'
(Left to Right) Brian Whyte, Jesse and Ray

Ray and his mom

Ray's mom and dad

Glory, Sherry, Ray and DJ - 1986

Glory's mom and dad with DJ and Sherry
They did a lot of babysitting as we were on tour
overseas and across Canada

Uncle Doug and his accordion
Ray still plays this accordion
every Christmas!

Ray enjoying a golf game…

DJ and Sherry-Rose
1981

Jimmy King singing "Saturday Night Fish Fry"
with daughters Chrystal and Cathy, Denis (guitar)
at Ray's 45th Birthday Party

Ray's son D.J.

Ray's daughter Cathy

Ray's Son Ray Jr.

Ray's daughter Sherry

*(Left to Right) grandsons - Jordon, Jeff, son-in-law – Rob,
granddaughter - Catie, daughter - Chrystal and
grandson - Cody*

*Ray and grandson
Cody*

Ray's Birthday Parties

*Ray's Annual Birthday Party – Oakbank,
Manitoba 1983*

Ray's Famous Birthday Parties at the Farm

Ray, Dr. Denis Hammerstedt and Warren Loose (Who wrote the poem to the song "The Old Leather Halter") at one of Ray's Annual Birthday Parties

Ray's Hawaiian Birthday Party

Ray's 65th Birthday Party!

Chrystal and D.J. performing at Ray's 65th Birthday party

Grandson Jordon at
65th Birthday Party

Ray at his 65th Birthday Party with friends Pat Nadeau, "Wild"
Bill Flamond, Jerilyn Shaneen, Hon. Eric Robinson, Ron
Nadeau and friends

Highlights of Ray's Career

Ray and Gary Buck viewing Ray's display at the
Country Music Hall of Fame in Calgary

Cathy, Ray, Glory and Eric Robinson, Honourable
Minister of Tourism, Heritage and Culture
Cathy (Ray's daughter) and Ray hosting the Manitoba Night for the
Juno Awards

Premier Gary Doer, 'Wild' Bill Flamond, Hon. Yvon Dumont, Ray
and Todd Lamirand

Ray 'voice of the Bear' Tipi Tales
by Lisa Meeches Productions on APTN

Ray and Lisa Meeches (Right)
2003 Toronto Skydome
Canadian Aboriginal Music Awards

Ray and NCI

Billboard on back of bus, 'Roadshow on NCI',
November, 2005

Ray 'on air' doing the Road Show

President of the Manitoba Metis Federation, David Chartrand and Ray 'on air', The Metis Hour X 2

Naomi Clark (co-host) and Ray,
The Metis Hour X2

Ray and special guest, Adam Beach,
Metis Hour X2

*Ron Nadeau, CEO NCI, Dave McLeod, General Manager, Ray and
'Wild' Bill Flamond, Senior Announcer
at the NCI golf tournament - 2005*

Ray St. Germain Country/Big Sky Country

1990 – 'Big Sky Country' Global TV
Ray Jr., Paul Pododworny, Angie Carriere, Ray,
Daryl Gutheil, Paul Kelly

'Ray St. Germain Country'
Suzanne Bird and Ray

'Ray St. Germain Country'
Sherisse Laurence and Stonewall Jackson
Global TV

'Ray St. Germain Country'
(Left to Right) Sherisse Laurence, Ray and
Jeannie C. Riley

(Left to right) Wendy Halldorson, daughters Chrystal, Cathy and Ray (Back Row) Denis Hammerstedt and Ron Halldorson on location 'Ray St. Germain Country' on Global TV, Dot and Les Loewen's Farm

'Ray St. Germain Country' taping at Lower Fort Garry - 1985

(Left to right) Ray's daughter Chrystal, Wendy Halldorson, Ray's daughter Cathy on 'Big Sky Country'

Joey Hollingsworth and Ray Toronto Airport 2003

Ray performing as Elvis

Tommy Hunter, Glory and Ray
Canadian Country Music Awards
Regina, Saskatchewan - 1981

Ray center stage singing 'The Metis' for the
North American Indigenous Games,
Winnipeg Stadium

NORTHERN TOUR

Beautiful accommodations up north

*The Northern Tour
Loading the plane*

Ready for take-off!

*Ray, Glory and children
coming to see the show*

Friends of the Family

Best Friends (Left to Right)
Les and Dot Loewen, Denis and Edith Hammerstedt, Paul
Bullock, Pat and Kas Siwik, Glory and Ray St. Germain,
Laureen "Sparky" Reeds (wife of Paul)

Glory and best friend
Laureen 'Sparky' Reeds

(Left to Right) Ray, Murray Parker, Arvel Gray and Glory
Ray took over Murray's Free Press route as a young boy
Murray claims Ray still owes him $2.00 for the bag

(Left to Right) Brent Edwards, Lorraine McCourt, Ray,
Michael McCourt and Murray Parker
Ray got a few broadcasting tips from Michael and Murray

Stan Thomas (Head of Programming CKND TV (Global))
wife Norma and Jimmy King

Ray and good friend Edie Reeves,
former V.P. of Warner Brothers
Records in Nashville
Dedication plaque to Edie Reeves